PROPHETIC
INVOCATIONS

THE
PROPHETIC
INVOCATIONS

COMPILED BY
ABDALLAH IBN ALAWI
AL-HADDAD

أذكار الصَّباح والمساء

للحَبيب عَبد الله بن عَلويّ الحدَّاد

CLARITAS
BOOKS

1 2 3 4 5 6 7 8 9 10

CLARITAS BOOKS

Bernard Street, Swansea, United Kingdom
Milpitas, California, United States

CLARITAS
BOOKS

First Published in June 2019

Typeset in Minion Pro 14/11

The Prophetic Invocations
Compiled by Abdallah Ibn Alawi al-Haddad
Translation, Transliteration, and Commentary by
Mostafa al-Badawi

A CIP catalogue record for this book is available from the British Library

ISBN: 978-1-905837-78-6

CONTENTS

Is it not through the remembrance of
God that heart find tranquillity?

—Quran 13:28

FOREWORD

IN THE NAME of God, the Most Merciful, the Compassionate. O God, we are incapable of praising You; You are as You have praised Yourself. All praise belongs to You alone. We ask You by Your Beautiful Names that You shower Your beloved Prophet with prayers and peace. May the blessings and peace of God be upon our master Muhammad, the unlettered Prophet, his family and wives, the mothers of the believers, and his descendants and Companions. May God's peace and blessings be upon all of them, as long as He is remembered by those who remember Him.

There is a well-known tradition related in Imam Malik's *Muwatta* that Jesus, the son of Mary, peace be upon them both, said, "Do not sit in a gathering without remembering God, for if you do, your hearts will harden, and a hard heart is distant from God." The hardening of the physical heart occurs from lack of physical exercise and from eating animal flesh with fat. Similarly, the spiritual heart is hardened by lack of spiritual exercise and eating the dead flesh of other humans (which is the metaphysical reality of the act of back-biting and slander).

The spiritual exercise of the heart is called "*dhikru'Llah*," which simply means, "remembering God." The practice of remembrance is a practice of recollecting another world and another time. When Odysseus came upon the Island of the Lotus-Eaters, some of his crew took one bite of the Lotus flower and were overcome with lethargy. As humans from all eras are wont to do, his crew forgot from whence they had come and that their journey was a return home. But one day all lotus-eaters must leave their dreams and wake up. "*Woe to us! Who has woken us from our sleep. This is just as the Most Merciful has promised, and the messengers have spoken the truth*" (36:52), say the sleepers of this world when they are finally and forcibly removed from the poppy field of pleasure and forgetfulness. The newly awoken come to the realisation that they were in fact accountable for every God-given breath, but they have squandered their entire lives foolishly or, worse still, spent them in malevolent deeds.

Breath is a Divine gift, and the tongue is the plane upon which the breezes of the breath blow. To speak, we need a tongue, lips, and breath. To remember God, we need a heart. We have been given all four and reminded by God in every Book of revelation that the reason we are created is to worship Him. In fact, everything in existence is initially created in a state of worship. However, because of their free will, humans can forget the reason for their existence. "And if you forget, remember," says the Quran.

It is through remembrance that equilibrium is established in the soul. *"Is it not by the remembrance of God that hearts are stilled?"* the Quran (13:28) rhetorically asks. This stillness is a result of several phenomena. The first is that when remembering God, one often feels His presence. While this may be true with the remembrance of anyone, the presence of God, as well as that of the Prophets and saints, brings a stillness of the heart without comparison.

Another cause for this stillness is the actual presence of angelic beings and the absence of the demonic, brought about by remembrance of God. In our modern world, we tend to shy away from mentioning unseen beings, such as angels and demons; but lack of belief in something does not necessitate its non-existence. Angels are real; they love the remembrance of God and will actually seek our places where He is being remembered in order to join in. Though unseen, their presence is felt by the worshipper.

Furthermore, the actual words themselves that are invoked to remember God bring stillness to the soul. Ancient languages produced an effect that more newly developed languages have not. For instance, when one hears Arabic, or sacerdotal Greek for that matter, one is struck by the power of the sounds even if the meanings are lost. This is certainly not true for most modern tongues. Arabic, in particular, has a special effect on the heart. For example, the simple yet most profound Islamic statement of creed, La ilaha illa'Llah, is composed of only three Arabic letters: alif, lam, and ha'. From these three letters, the words for "no," "god," "except," and the Divine name "Allah" are derived.

These letters are pronounced simply by moving the tongue up and down, lightly touching the roof of the mouth. In ancient Chinese medicine, this action of the tongue was believed to unify all of the meridian channels in the body and engender good health. In addition, throughout the first few years of life, an infant will commonly place its tongue on the roof of its mouth and bring it back down.

While these are interesting facts, there is a more fundamental reason why remembrance of God affects us in such a positive way. Simply stated, the entire body craves Divine remembrance more intensely than anything else. Every cell in the body is individually in a state of remembrance. When the heart and its translator, the tongue, join in, harmony occurs.

There is no doubt that meditation and prayer from traditions other than Islam also have an effect. Many people experience physical benefits, such as lower blood pressure, less stress, and better sleep. What Islamic spiritual practice offers additionally is a pure, unadulterated tradition. Its authenticity is guaranteed due to its direct connection to its original sources preserved by an unbroken chain of transmitters.

When I was a young student of the New Testament at a Jesuit high school, my teacher, a brilliant Jesuit priest, Father Daugherty said, "I can guarantee only two words in the entire New Testament were uttered by Jesus," upon him be peace, "and they are *Abba* and *Amen*!" However, the primary sources of Islam have been rigorously authenticated and are unlike those of other religions in this respect. Thus, we can be absolutely certain that the formulas found in this book were uttered by our beloved Prophet ﷺ and were passed on to us, his community, for protection and peace. We need these prayers for our sanity and for our protection from the evils of the world.

The compiler of this text is the great Imam, Shaykh Abdallah lbn Alawi al-Haddad, a direct descendent of the Prophet Muhammad ﷺ from both sides of his family as well as from the well-known and loved clan of Ba 'Alawi of Hadramawt, Yemen. Our Prophet ﷺ said, "Toward the end of time, take to the people of Sham (Greater Syria), and if not them, then the people of Yemen." Today, it is acknowledged that the last two great bastions of traditional Islam on the Peninsula of Arabia Felix are Yemen and Sham. While there are some great scholars left in the Indian Subcontinent and in the Western lands of Islam, such as Chinqit (Sub-Saharan Africa) and Mali, the majority of traditional scholars lie buried in the earth, and their books remain neglected.

This text is small but powerful in that it draws its words from the pure sunna (words, deeds, and actions) of the Prophet Muhammad ﷺ who remembered God in all of his states. The Quran, in turn, praises those who remember God: *Remember Me, and I will remember you* (2:152); *Those who let neither buying nor selling divert them from the remembrance of God ... God shall reward them for the best of what they did, and increase them in reward from His bounty* (24:37-38); *The believers are those who when the name of God is mentioned their hearts tremble ... They will have degrees of rank with their Lord and forgiveness and generous provision* (8:2-4). There is not a page in the Quran that does not have some reminder for us; indeed, the entire Quran is a reminder.

The text is a *wird*, which is commonly translated as "litany." *Wird* literally means "a place of water," and this meaning is telling. A watering place is visited regularly not out of mere fondness but out of necessity. The spiritual aspirant should approach his *wird* with the same thirst and regularity he would his watering place. As water satisfies the body's physical demand, so too does the *wird* bring the soul to a state of contentment and, eventually, delight. The Quran is itself a *wird*, a portion of which should be recited by Muslims daily.

This edition is distinguished by the fact that its translator, Dr. Mostafa al-Badawi, spent a large part of his adult life in the company and under the guidance of Shaykh Ahmad Mashhur al-Haddad, who was a direct descendent of the complier of this *wird* and also himself a master of the inner and outer sciences of Islam. While this is a general *wird* that can be used without the supervision of a spiritual physician, I personally had the blessing of taking this *wird* from Shaykh Ahmad al-Haddad, may God be pleased with him, during his blessed life of scholarship and spiritual guidance. In one blessed gathering held by the Shaykh, may God be pleased with him, he told me that now is the age of *hawsat*. I did not know the meaning of this word and asked him what it meant. He replied, "Mental instability as a result of leaving the remembrance of God."

This *wird* is a healing and Prophetic medicine from a doctor of the hearts, Imam Abdallah al-Haddad, who learned his craft from true scholars of knowledge and deeds, until he himself became a master. According to an authentic hadith, "Scholars are the heirs of the prophets," and an heir, as any Islamic jurist knows, is able to use the inheritance according to his own discretion. Thus, the scholars of this Islamic community are the heirs of the last of God's prophets, the paragon of His creation, our master Muhammad ﷺ. Imam Abdallah al-Haddad was such an heir and has presented this text, blessed by virtue of being composed entirely of Divine and prophetic revelation, and arranged as none but a master physician can be trusted to arrange. What is left for us is only to take the medicine.

As the poet said: "*We heal ourselves with Your remembrance, and should we forget, we are in relapse.*"

—HAMZA YUSUF

الورد اللَّطيف

Al-Wird al-Latif

INTRODUCTION

I MAM ABDALLAH AL-HADDAD is a well-known Alawi scholar from Hadramawt. To say Alawi is to say Husayni in lineage[1], Ash'ari in *aqida*[2] Shafi'i in *fiqh*[3], and Ghazali in behaviour. As with other illustrious Alawis, God made him known despite his wish to remain in obscurity. Yet the Imam once said to some of his close disciples that what they saw as fame was in fact not so, for had he really wished for fame and requested it from God, he would have easily eclipsed all other scholars and saints on the face of the earth.

Imam al-Haddad was born in Tarim, Yemen, in 1044 AH, and by the time he was about thirty years of age, had already acquired the reputation of being the foremost scholar and godly person of his time.

His main litany was al-*Wird al-Kabir,* which he recited twice daily, after Dawn (Fajr) and Sunset (*Maghrib*) Prayers. Also his were the *Ratib, Hizb al-Fath*, and *Hizb al-Nasr. Hizb al-Fath* is concerned with purifying the heart by getting rid of the rust covering it, then acquiring virtues and practicing them to the full, hence its name: "*The Litany of the Opening.*" *Hizb al-Nasr*, "Litany of Victory," was designed for protection against outward and inward enemies.

Al-*Wird al-Kabir* being rather lengthy, the Imam composed a meaning. In this, as in his books and spiritual instruction, the Imam foresaw the time when people would have neither the time nor the will to do all that was required. *Al-Wird al-Latif* was therefore made for us, in this 15th century *Hijra*. It is short, taking no more than fifteen minutes to complete, once one has become familiar with it, and it is to be recited after *Fajr* and *Maghrib*. If this is not possible, it is to be recited once before and once after midday, whenever time is available.

This present work is intended to help the English speaker familiarise himself with the meanings of various prophetic invocations of the *wird* and some of their merits and benefits, in a format geared toward recitation. This transliteration is meant to be the nearest possible rendering of the actual vocal recitation. A word like *Nabiyyan*, for instance, when it comes at the end of a sentence, is pronounced *Nabiyya*, so this is how it has been transliterated.

Arabic differs from other languages in its being the language of the Quran, the language that God chose to make worthy of conveying His revelation. Revelation is eternal knowledge of reality expressed in human languages. Its vehicle requires exceptional precision, depth, subtlety, and malleability to render it adequate for the purpose. Furthermore, the manner in which God and, to a leaser extent, His Messenger ﷺ use the language is of an altogether different order from its other usages. A single verse of the Quran will have many superimposed layers of meaning. It may be used for protection from various inward and outward perils, for curing certain illnesses, for increasing certain kinds of provision, for *Baraka [blessings]*, and for the recompense promised for the recitation of each of its letters.

Knowing this, Muslims all over the world have always recited both the Quran and the Prophetic invocations in their original Arabic, even when unable to understand the language, in order to make sure that they lose none of the secrets and *baraka*, much of which are lost in translation.

However, prayer is not limited to specific times or occasions; it is a constant communication with God. Whenever we leave our house or cross the street, we ask God for protection. When hungry we ask Him to feed us and when worried to reassure us. This kind of spontaneous prayer should not be subject to constraints of language or even style. The companions of the Prophet ﷺ felt entirely free to address their petitions to God in their own words, or in the case of a bedouin, in his local dialects, despite having memorised the Prophet's words and making frequent use of them.

As with all litanies of Imam al-Haddad, *al-Wird al-Latif* is made up of nothing but the prayers of the Prophet ﷺ and the formulas that he instructed his community to recite mornings and evenings. It is, therefore, strictly in conformity with the *sunna*, and once it is well rehearsed and becomes a habit, one can rest assured that he or she is following the Prophetic instructions as to what invocations he should use to begin and end his day.

NOTES

1. The Alawi lineage is the most authentic of all *sharifian* lineages. Each Alawi knows precisely who his ancestors were, up to Imam Husayn, the Prophet's grandson.

2. Imam Abu'l-Hasan al-Ash'ari formulated the creed of Ahl al-Sunna wal-Jama'a, and his formulation remains, together with Imam Abu Mansur al-Maturidi's, that of the great majority of Muslims today.

3. Soon after the arrival of their ancestor, Imam Ahmad ibn Isa, from Iraq to Hadramawt, the Alawis adopted the Shafi'i madhhab in all matters of jurisprudence. They are most insistent on the importance of acquiring a solid foundation in fiqh, for women and men.

4. When they saw Imam al-Ghazali's Ihya' 'Ulum al-Din, (Revival of the Religious Sciences), the Alawi's found that the shaykh had made a full exposition of everything they wished to teach. They therefore adopted the Ihya' as their main teaching book in matters of tasawwuf, which, in their view, is the practice of Shariah with the utmost sincerity and the purification of the heart from all its ailments.

ARABIC & TRANSLATION

1)   بِسْمِ اللَّهِ الرَّحْمَٰنِ الرَّحِيمِ

قُلْ هُوَ ٱللَّهُ أَحَدٌ (١) ٱللَّهُ ٱلصَّمَدُ (٢) لَمْ يَـــلِدْ وَلَمْ يُولَـــدْ (٣) وَلَمْ يَكُـن لَّـهُ كُفُـواً أَحَدٌ (٤) (ثلاثاً)

In the name of Allah, the most Merciful, the Compassion- ate. Say: He, Allah, is One. Allah is the eternally Besought. He has not begotten, nor been begotten, and equal to Him there is none. (112)

٢) بِسْمِ اللَّهِ الرَّحْمَنِ الرَّحِيمِ

قُـلْ أَعُوذُ بِـرَبِّ الفَلَقِ (١) مِـن شَرِّ مَـا خَلَـقَ (٢) وَمِـن شَرِّ غَاسِـقٍ إِذَا وَقَـبَ (٣) وَمِـن شَرِّ النَّفَّـٰثَـٰتِ فِي ٱلْعُقَـدِ (٤) وَمِـن شَرِّ حَاسِـدٍ إِذَا حَسَـدَ (٥) (ثلاثاً)

In the Name of Allah, the Most Merciful, the Compassion-ate. Say: I take refuge with the Lord of the daybreak; from the evil of what He has created; from the evil of darkness when it gathers; from the evil of the women who blow on knots; and from the evil of an envier when he envies. (113)

٣) بِسْمِ اللَّهِ الرَّحْمَنِ الرَّحِيمِ

قُـلْ أَعُـوذُ بِـرَبِّ ٱلنَّـاسِ (١) مَلِـكِ ٱلنَّـاسِ (٢) إِلَـٰهِ ٱلنَّـاسِ (٣) مِـن شَرِّ ٱلْوَسْوَاسِ ٱلْخَنَّاسِ (٤) ٱلَّـذِي يُوَسْوِسُ فِي صُدُورِ ٱلنَّـاسِ (٥) مِنَ ٱلْجِنَّـةِ وَٱلنَّـاسِ (٦) (ثلاثاً)

In the Name of Allah, the Most Merciful, the Compassionate. Say: I take refuge with the Lord of men; the King of men; the God of men; from the evil of the withdrawing whisperer; who whispers in the breasts of men; of jinn and men. (114)

4) بِسْمِ اللَّهِ الرَّحْمَنِ الرَّحِيمِ

رَبِّ أَعُوذُ بِكَ مِنْ هَمَزَاتِ ٱلشَّيَاطِينِ (٩٧) وَأَعُوذُ بِكَ رَبِّ أَن يَحْضُرُونِ (٩٨) (ثَلَاثاً)

My Lord! I seek Your protection against the insinuations of the devils and I seek your protection against their approaching me. (23:97-98)

5) أَفَحَسِبْتُمْ أَنَّمَا خَلَقْنَاكُمْ عَبَثاً وَأَنَّكُمْ إِلَيْنَا لَا تُرْجَعُونَ (١١٥) فَتَعَالَى ٱللَّهُ ٱلْمَلِكُ ٱلْحَقُّ لَا إِلَـهَ إِلَّا هُوَ رَبُّ ٱلْعَرْشِ ٱلْكَرِيمِ (١١٦) وَمَن يَدْعُ مَعَ ٱللَّهِ إِلَـهاً ءَاخَرَ لَا بُرْهَـنَ لَهُ بِهِ فَإِنَّمَا حِسَابُهُ عِندَ رَبِّهِ إِنَّهُ لَا يُفْلِحُ الْكَـفِرُونَ (١١٧) وَقُل رَّبِّ ٱغْفِرْ وَ ٱرْحَمْ وَأَنتَ خَيْرُ ٱلرَّاحِمِينَ (١١٨)

What, did you think that We created you in vain, and that to Us you should not be returned? But Exalted is Allah, the King, the Real, there is no god but He, the Lord of the Throne, the Generous. And whosoever calls upon another god with Allah of which he has no proof, his reckoning is with his Lord; the disbelievers never succeed. And say: My Lord! Forgive and have mercy, for You are the Most Merciful. (23:115-118)

(6) فَسُبْحَـٰنَ اللَّهِ حِينَ تُمْسُونَ وَحِينَ تُصْبِحُونَ (١٧) وَلَهُ ٱلْحَمْدُ فِى ٱلسَّمَـٰوَٰتِ وَٱلْأَرْضِ وَعَشِيًّا وَحِينَ تُظْهِرُونَ (١٨) يُخْرِجُ ٱلْحَىَّ مِنَ ٱلْمَيِّتِ وَيُخْرِجُ ٱلْمَيِّتَ مِنَ ٱلْحَىِّ وَ يُحْـى ٱلْأَرْضَ بَعْدَ مَوْتِهَا وَكَذَٰلِكَ تُخْرَجُونَ (١٩)

So glorify Allah when evening comes upon you and when morning comes upon you. To Him belongs all praise in the heavens and the earth. [Glorify Him] in the evenings and high noon. He brings forth the living from the dead, and He brings forth the dead from the living, and He revives the earth after it is dead; even so you shall be brought forth. (30:17-19)

(7) أَعُوذُ بِاللهِ السَّمِيعِ العَلِيمِ مِنَ الشَّيْطَانِ الرَّجِيمِ (ثلاثا) *

I seek Allah's protection, Who is the Hearer, the Knower, from the repudiate Devil.

(8) لَوْ أَنزَلْنَا هَـٰذَا ٱلْقُرْءَانَ عَلَىٰ جَبَلٍ لَّرَأَيْتَهُ خَـٰشِعًا مُّتَصَدِّعًا مِّنْ خَشْيَةِ ٱللَّهِ وَتِلْكَ ٱلْأَمْثَـٰلُ نَضْرِبُهَا لِلنَّاسِ لَعَلَّهُمْ يَتَفَكَّرُونَ (٢١) هُوَ ٱللَّهُ ٱلَّذِى لَآ إِلَـٰهَ إِلَّا هُوَ عَـٰلِمُ ٱلْغَيْبِ وَٱلشَّهَـٰدَةِ هُوَ ٱلرَّحْمَـٰنُ ٱلرَّحِيمُ (٢٢) هُوَ ٱللَّهُ ٱلَّذِى لَآ إِلَـٰهَ إِلَّا هُوَ ٱلْمَلِكُ ٱلْقُدُّوسُ ٱلسَّلَـٰمُ ٱلْمُؤْمِنُ ٱلْمُهَيْمِنُ ٱلْعَزِيزُ ٱلْجَبَّارُ ٱلْمُتَكَبِّرُ سُبْحَـٰنَ ٱللَّهِ عَمَّا يُشْرِكُونَ (٢٣) هُوَ

اَللَّهُ الْخَــالِقُ الْبَارِئُ الْمُصَوِّرُ لَهُ الْأَسْمَاءُ الْحُسْنَىٰ يُسَبِّحُ لَهُ مَا فِى السَّمَٰوَٰتِ وَالْأَرْضِ وَ هُوَ الْعَزِيزُ الْحَكِيمُ (٢٤)

Had We sent down this Quran upon a mountain, you would have seen it humbled, split asunder out of the fear of Allah. And those examples, We strike them for people that they may reflect. He is Allah; there is no god but He. He is the Knower of the unseen and the visible; He is the All-Merciful the Compassionate. He is Allah; there is no god but He. He is the King, the Holy, the Peace, the Faithful, the Sovereign, the Eminent, the Compeller, the Proud. Transcendent is Allah beyond what they associate. He is Allah, the Creator, the Fashioner, the Shaper. To Him belong the Most Beautiful Names. All that is in the heavens and the earth magnifies Him. He is the August, the Wise. (59:21-24)

(9) سَلَـٰمٌ عَلَىٰ نُوحٍ فِى الْعَـٰلَمِينَ (٧٩) إِنَّا كَذَٰلِكَ نَجْزِى الْمُحْسِنِينَ (٨٠) إِنَّهُ مِنْ عِبَادِنَا الْمُؤْمِنِينَ (٨١)

Peace be upon Noah among all beings. This is how We recompense those who excel, he was one of Our believing slaves. (37:79-81)

10)   أَعُوذُ بِكَلِماتِ اللهِ التَّامَّاتِ مِن شَرِّ مَا خَـلَقَ (ثَلاثا) *

I take refuge in the complete words of Allah from the evil in what He has created.

11)   بِسـمِ اللهِ الَّـذِي لا يَـضُرُّ مَـعَ اسْـمِـهِ شَـيْءٌ في الأَرضِ ولا في السَّـمَاءِ ، وَهُـوَ السَّـمِيعُ العَلِيـمُ (ثَلاثا) *

In the Name of Allah, with Whose Name nothing on earth or in heaven can harm. He is the Hearer, the Knower.

12)   اللَّهُـمَّ إِنِّي أَصْبَـحْتُ مِنْكَ في نِعْمَةٍ وَعَافِيَةٍ وَسِتْرٍ، فَأَتِـمَّ عَـلَيَّ نِعْمَتَـكَ وَعَافِيَتَـكَ وَسِـتْرَكَ في الدُّنْيَا وَالآخِرَةِ (ثَلاثا) *

O Allah! As Morning comes upon me I dwell in Your favour, well-being, and protection, so complete Your favour upon me, Your well-being and Your protection, in this world and the next!

13)   اللَّهُـمَّ إنِّي أَصْبَـحْتُ أُشْهِـدُكَ ، وَأُشْـهِـدُ حَمَلَـةَ عَرْشِـكَ ، وَمَلائكَتَكَ ، وَجَمِيعَ خَلْـقِكَ ، أَنَّـكَ أَنْتَ اللهُ لا إله إلا أَنْتَ وَحْدَكَ لا شَرِيـكَ لَـكَ ، وَأَنَّ مُحَمَّـداً عَبْدُكَ وَرَسُولُـكَ (أربعاً) *

O Allah! As morning comes upon me, I bear witness before You and before the Carriers of Your Throne, and Your angels, and all Your creation, that You are Allah , that there is no god but You, Alone, with no partners, and that Muhammad is Your slave and messenger.

14) الْحَمْـدُ للـهِ رَبِّ الْعَالَمِـين، حَمْـداً يُـوَافِي نِعَمَـهُ وَيُكَافِـئُ مَزِيـدَه (ثلاثاً)*

Praise and thanks be to Allah, Lord of the Worlds, with a praise that is adequate to His favours and equal to His increase.

15) آمَنْـتُ بِاللَّـهِ الْعَظِيـم ، وَكَفَـرْتُ بِالْجِبْـتِ وَالطَّاغُـوت، وَاسْتَمْسَكْتُ بِالْعُـرْوَةِ الْوُثْقَـى، لَا انْفِصَامَ لَهَا، وَاللهُ سَـمِيعٌ عَلِيـم (ثلاثاً)*

I believe in Allah the Formidable, and I denounce the idols and the sorcerers, and I hold fast to the firmest handhold, that which does not break, and Allah is Hearer and Knower.

16) رَضِيْـتُ بِاللـهِ رَبّـاً، وَبِالإِسْلام دِينـاً، وَبِسَيِـدِنَا مُحَمَّـدٍ صَلَّـي

اللـهُ عَلَيـهِ وَسَلَّمَ، نَبِيَّاً وَرَسُـولاً (ثلاثاً)*

I am content with Allah as Lord, with Islam as religion, and with our master Muhammad, may Allah's blessings and peace be upon him, as Prophet and Messenger.

(17)   حَسْـبِيَ اللـهُ لا إِلـهَ إِلّا هُـوَ، عَلَيـهِ تَوَكَّـلْتُ،وَهُوَ رَبُّ العَـرْشِ العَظِـيمِ (سـبعاً)*

Allah is my sufficiency; there is no god but He. On Him do I rely; He is the Formidable Lord of the Throne.

(18)   اللّهُمَّ صَلَّ عَلى سَيِّدِنا مُحَمَّدٍ وَآلِهِ وصَحْبِهِ وَسَلِّم (عشرا)*

O Allah! Bless our master Muhammad, his Family and Companions, and give them peace.

(19)   اللّهُمَّ إِنِّي أَسْأَلُكَ مِنْ فَجَاءَةِ الْخَيرِ، وَأَعُوذُ بِكَ مِنْ فَجَاءَةِ الشَّرِّ*

O Allah! I ask You for sudden good and seek Your protection from sudden evil.

(20) اللَّهُمَّ أَنْتَ رَبِّي، لا إِلَه إلا أَنت، خَلَقْتَنِي وَأَنَا عَبْدُك، وَأَنَا عَلَى عَهْدِكَ وَوَعْدِكَ مَا اسْتَطَعْتُ، أَعُوذُ بِكَ مِنْ شَرِّ مَا صنعت، أَبُوءُ لَكَ بِنِعْمَتِكَ عَلَيَّ وَأَبُوءُ بِذَنْبِي، فَاغْفِرْ لي، فَإِنَّهُ لا يَغْفِرُ الذُّنُوبَ إلا أَنتَ*

O Allah! You are my Lord, there is no god but You, You created me and I am Your slave, I uphold your pledge and promise as well as I can; I seek Your protection against the evil that I have done; I acknowledge Your favours upon me and I acknowledge my sin, so forgive me, for none forgives sin except You.

(21) اللَّهُمَّ أَنْتَ رَبِّي لَا إِلَهَ إِلَّا أَنت، عَلَيكَ تَوَكَّلتُ، وَأَنْتَ رَبُّ الْعَرْش الْعَظِيمِ*

O Allah! You are my Lord, there is no god but You, upon You do I rely, and You are the Lord of the Throne, the For-midable

(22) مَا شَاءَ اللهُ كَانَ وَمَا لَمْ يَشَأْ لَمْ يَكُن، ولَا حَوْلَ وَلَا قُوَّةَ إِلَّا بِاللَّهِ الْعَلِيِّ الْعَظِيمِ*

What Allah wishes happens, what He does not does not;
there is neither power nor ability save by Allah, the High,
the Formidable.

أَعْلَمُ أَنَّ اللهَ عَلَى كُلِّ شَيْءٍ قَدِيرٍ، وَأَنَّ اللّهَ قَدْ أَحَاطَ بِكُلِّ (23)
شَيْءٍ عِلْما*

I know that Allah has power over all things and that Allah
encompasses all things in His knowledge.

اللَّهُمَّ إِنِّي أَعُوذُ بِكَ مِنْ شَرِّ نَفْسِي وَ مِنْ شَرِّ كُلِّ دَابَّةٍ أَنْتَ (24)
آخِذٌ بِنَاصِيَتِهَا، إِنَّ رَبِّي عَلَى صِرَاطٍ مُسْتَقِيمٍ*

O Allah! I seek Your protection from the evil of my soul
and the evil of every creature on earth You have taken by
the forehead; my Lord is on a straight path.

يَا حَيُّ يَا قَيُّومُ، بِرَحْمَتِكَ أَسْتَغِيثُ، وَمِنْ عَذَابِكَ أَسْتَجِيرُ، (25)
أَصْلِحْ لِي شَأْنِي كُلَّهُ، وَلَا تَكِلْنِي إِلَى نَفْسِي وَلَا إِلَى أَحَدٍ مِنْ خَلْقِكَ
طَرْفَةَ عَيْنٍ*

O Living! O Sustainer! I call upon Your mercy for succour,

and from Your chastisement I seek refuge! Make good all my affairs and do not entrust me to myself or any of Your creation for the blink of an eye.

(26) اللَّهُـمَّ إِنِّي أَعُـوذُ بِـكَ مِـنَ الْهَـمِّ وَالْحَـزَنِ، وَأَعُـوذُ بِـكَ مِـنْ الْعَجْـزِ وَالْكَسَـلِ، وَأَعُـوذُ بِـكَ مِـنْ الْجُـبْنِ وَالْبُخْـلِ، وَأَعُـوذُ بِـكَ مِـنْ غَلَـبَةِ الدَّيْـنِ، وَقَهْـرِ الرِّجَـالِ *

O Allah! I seek Your protection from sorrow and grief, and I seek Your protection from incapacity and sloth, and I seek Your protection from cowardice and avarice, and I seek Your protection from the stress of debts and the tyranny of men.

(27) اللَّهُـمَّ إِنِّي أَسْأَلُـكَ العَفْوَ وَالعافِيَةَ وَالمُعَافَاةَ الدَّائِمَةَ في دَيْنِي وَدُنْـيايَ وَأَهْـلِي وَمالِي *

O Allah! I ask of You pardon, well-being, and constant safety in my religion, worldly life, family, and possessions.

(28) اللَّهُـمَّ اسْتُرْ عوْراتي وآمِنْ رَوْعاتي *

O Allah! Cover my shameful things and assuage my fears.

(29) اللّٰهُـمَّ احْفَظْنِـي مِـن بَـيـن يَـدَيَّ وَمِن خَلْفِـي، وَعَـن يَمِينِـي وَعَـن شِمالِي، وَمِن فَوْقِـي، وَأَعـوذُ بِعَظَمَتِكَ أَن أُغْـتالَ مِـن تَحْتِـي *

O Allah! Protect me from [the evil that comes from] in front of me, from behind my back, my right, my left, and from above me and I take refuge in Your Greatness from unexpected harm from below me.

(30) اللّٰهُـمَّ أَنـتَ خَلَقْتَنِـي وَأَنـتَ تَهْدِينِـي، وَأَنـتَ تُطعِمُنِـي وَأَنـتَ تَسْـقِينِي، وَأَنـتَ تُمِيثُنِـي وَأَنـتَ تُحْيِينِـي *

O Allah! You created me and You guide me, and You provide me with food and You provide me with drink, and You cause me to die and You give me life.

(31) أَصْبَحْنـا عَـلَى فِطْرَةِ الإسْلام، وَعَـلَى كَلِمَـةِ الإخْـلاَص، وَعَـلَى دِيـنِ نَبِيِّنـا مُحَمَّـدٍ، صَـلَّى اللَّـه عَلَيْـهِ وَآلِـهِ وَسَـلَّم، وَعَـلَى مِلَّـةِ أَبِينـا إبْراهِيـم، حَنِيفـاً، مُسْـلِماً، وَمَا كَانَ مِـنَ الـمُشْرِكِينَ *

We have risen this morning on the original pattern of Islam, on the Word of Sincerity, on the religion of our Prophet Muhammad, may Allah bless him and his family and grant them peace, and on the confession of Ibrahim, who was upright, a Muslim, and not an idolator.

(32) اللّهُـمَّ بِـكَ أَصْـبَحْنَا، وَبِـكَ أَمْسَـينا، وَبِـكَ نَحْـيَا، وَبِـكَ
نَمُـوتُ، وَإِلَـيْكَ النُّـشُـورُ *
(وَيقُـولُ فِي الـمَسَاءِ: وَإِلَيْكَ الَمصير)

O Allah! You made us live this morning and You made us live this evening. You Make us alive and you make us die, and to You is the arising. [In the evening: '… and to You is the final end.']

(33) أَصْـبَحْنا وَأَصْـبَحَ الـمُـلْكُ للّه، الَحَمْـدُ للـه رَبِّ آلَعَالَمِـين *
(وَيقُـولُ فِي الـمَسَاءِ: أَمْسَـينَا وَأَمْـسَى الـمُلْكُ)

Morning has risen upon us and sovereignty is all Allah's and all praises and thanks belong to Allah, Lord of the Worlds. [In the evening: 'Evening has fallen upon us and sovereignty is all Allah's…']

(34)   اللّهُـمَّ إِنِّي أَسْأَلُكَ خَـيْـرَ هـذَا اليَـوْمِ، فَتْحَـهُ، وَنَـصْرَهُ، وَنـورَهُ، وَبَرَكَتَـهُ، وَهُـدَاهُ *
(وَيَقُولُ فِي المَسَاءِ : هذِهِ اللَّيَلَةِ)

O Allah! I ask You the good of this day, its openings, victo-
ries, lights, blessings, and right-guidance. [In the evening
replace 'day' with 'night']

(35)   اللّهُـمَّ إِنِّي أَسْأَلُكَ خَـيْـرَ هَـذَا اليَـوْمِ وَخَـيْـرَ مَـا فِيهِ، وأَعـوذُ بِـكَ مِـنْ شَرِّ هَـذَاَ اليَـوْمِ وَمِـنْ شَرِّ مَـا فِيهِ *   (و يَقـول فِي المَسَـاءِ : هـذِهِ اللَّيْلَـةِ)

O Allah! I ask of You the good of this day and the best of
what is in it, and I seek Your protection against the evil of
this day and the worst of what is in it. (In the evening replace 'day' with 'night.')

(36)   اللّهُـمَّ مَـا أَصْبَـحَ بِي مِـنْ نِعْمَـة أَوْ بِأَحَـد مِـنْ خَلْقِكَ فَمِنْكَ وَحْدَكَ لَا شَرِيكَ لَك، فَلَكَ الْحَمْدُ وَلَكَ الشُّكْرُ عَلَي ذلِكَ * (وَيَقُولُ فِي المَسَـاءِ : اللّهُـمَّ مَـا أَمْـسى)

O Allah! Whatever favours I, or any of Your creatures, received this morning, they come only from You; You have no associates, so Yours are the praises and Yours are the thanks for them all. [In the evening replace 'this morning' with 'to-night.']

(37)   سُبْحَانَ اللهِ وَبِحَمْدِهِ (مائة مرَّة)*

Transcendent is Allah and by His praises!

(38)   سُبْحَانَ اللهِ الْعَظِيمِ وَبِحَمْدِهِ (مائة مرَّة)*

Transcendent is Allah the Formidable and by His Praises!

(39)   سُبْحَانَ اللهِ، وَالْحَمْدُ لِلَّهِ، وَلَا إِلَهَ إِلا اللَّهُ، وَاللَّهُ أَكْبَرُ (مائة مـرَّة)*

Transcendent is Allah, all praise belongs to Allah, there is no deity other than Allah, Allah is the Greater.

(40)   وَيَزِيدُ صَبَاحاً: لَا إِلَهَ إِلَّا اللهُ وَحْدَهُ لَا شَرِيكَ لَهُ، لَهُ الـمُلْكُ وَلَهُ الحَمْدُ، وَ هُـوَ عَـلَى كُلِّ شَيْءٍ قَدِير(مائـة مـرَّة)*

And to be added in the morning: There is no god but Allah alone, with no partners, His is sovereignty, His is all praise, and He is powerful over all things.

TRANSLITERATION

1. BismiLlahi'r-Rahmani'r-Rahim. Qul huwa'Llahu Ahad, Allahu's-Samad, lam yalid, wa lam yulad, wa lam yakun laHu kufuwan ahad. [3 times]

2. Qul a'udhu birabbi'l-falaq; min sharri ma khalaq; wa min sharri ghasiqin idha waqab; wa min shar-ri'n-naffathati fil-'uqad; wa min sharri hasidin idha hasad. [3 times]

3. Qul a'udhu birabbi'n-nas; maliki'n-nas; ilahi'n-nas; min sharri'l-waswasi'l-khannas; alladhi yuwaswisu fi suduri'n-nas; min'al-jinnati wa'n-nas. [3 times]

4. Rabbi a'udhu bika min hamazati'sh-shayatini wa a 'udhu bika rabbi an yahdurun. [3 times]

5. Afahasibtum annama khalaqnakum 'abathan wa annakum ilayna la turja'un; fata'ala'Llahu'l-Mali-ku'l-Haqqu la ilaha illa huwa Rabbu'l-'Arshil-karim.

Wa man yad'u ma'a'Llahi ilahan akhara la burhana
lahu bihi fa'innama hisabuhu 'inda Rabbihi, innahu
la yuflihu'l-kafirun. Wa qul Rabbi'ghfir wa'rham wa
Anta khayru'r-Rahimin.

6. Fasubhana'Llahi hina tumsuna wa hina tusbihun; wa
    lahu'l-hamdu fi's-samawati wal-ardi wa 'ashiyyan wa
    hina tudhirun; yukhriju'l- hayya mina'l-mayyiti, wa
    yukhriju'l-mayyita mina'l- hay, wa yuhyi'l-arda ba'da
    mawtiha, wa kadhalika tukhrajun. [3 times]

7. A'udhu bi'Llahi's-Sami'i'l-'Alimi mina'sh-shaytani'r-rajim.
    [3 times]

8. Law anzalna hadha'l-Qurana 'ala jabalin lar'ayta-
    hu khashi'an mutasaddi'an min khashyati'Llah;
    wa tilka'l-amthalu nadribuha li'n-nasi la'Allahum
    yatafakkarun. Huwa'Llahu'lladhi la ilaha ila Huwa,
    'Alimu'l-ghaybi wa'sh-shahadati, Huwa'r-Rahma-
    ni'r-Rahim. Huwa'Llahu'lladhi la ilaha illa Huwa,
    al-Maliku'l-Quddusu's-Salamu'l-Mu'minu'l-Mu-
    hayminu'l-'Azizu'l-Jabbaru'l-Mutakabbir; subha-
    na'Llahi 'amma yushrikun. Huwa 'Llahu'I-Khaliqu
    l-Bari'ul-Musawwir, laHu'l-Asma'ul-husna, yusabbihu
    lahu ma fi's-samawati wa'l-ardi wa Huwal-Azizu

'l-Hakim.

9. Salamun 'ala Nuhin fi'l-alamin inna kadhalika na-jzi'l-muhsinin, innahu min 'ibadina'l-mu'minin.

10. A'udhu bi kalimati'Llahi't-tammati min sharri ma khalaq. [3 times]

11. BismiLlahi'lladhi la yadurru ma'asmihi shay'un fi'l-ardi wa la fi's-sama'i, wa huwa's-Sami'u'l-Alim. [3 times]

12. Allahumma inni asbahtu minka fi ni'matin wa 'afiya-tin wa sitr; fa'timma ni'mataka 'alayya wa 'afiyataka wa sitraka fi'd-dunya wa'l-akhira. [3 times]

13. Allahumma inni asbahtu ush-hiduka, wa ush-hi-du hamalata 'arshika, wa mala'ikataka, wa jami'a khalqiqa, annaka anta'Llahu, la ilaha illa anta, wahdaka la sharika laka, wa anna Muhammadan 'abduka wa rasuluk. [4 times]

14. Al-hamdu lia'Llhi Rabbi'l-alamin, hamdan yuwafi ni'amahu wa yukafi'u mazidah. [3 times]

15. Amantu biLlahi'l-'Adhim, wa kafartu bi'l-jibti wa't-taghut, wa'stamsaktu bi'l-'urwati'l-wuthqa, la'nfisima laha, wAllahu Sami'un, 'Alim. [3 times]

16. Raditu biLlahi Rabban, wa bi'l-Islami dinan, wa

bi sayyidina Muhammadin, salla'Llahu 'alayhi wa
sallama, nabiyyan wa rasula. [3 times]

17. Hasbiya'Llahu la ilaha illa Huwa, 'alayhi tawakkaltu,
wa Huwa Rabbu'l-'Arshi'l-'Adhim [7 times]

18. Allahumma salli 'ala sayyidina Muhammadin wa
alihi wa sahbihi wa sallim. [10 times]

19. Allahumma inni as'aluka min fuja'at'il-khayri, wa
a'uadhu bika min fuja'at'ish-sharr.

20. Allahumma anta Rabbi, la ilaha illa ant, khalaqtani
wa ana 'abduk, wa ana 'ala 'ahdika wa wa'dika
ma'stata't, a'udhu bika min sharri ma sana't, abu'u
laka bini' matika 'alaya wa abu'u bi dhanbi, fa'ghfir li,
fa'innahu la yaghfiru'dh-dhunuba illa ant.

21. Allahumma anta Rabbi, la ilaha illa ant, 'alayka
tawakkaltu, wa anta Rabb'ul-'Arshi'l-'Adhim.

22. Ma sha'Allahu kana, wa ma lam yasha' lam yakun,
wa la hawla wa la quwwata illa bi'Llahi'l- Ali-
yy'l-'Adhim

23. A'lamu anna'Llaha 'ala kulli shay'in qadir, wa anna'Llaha qad ahata bi kulli shay'in 'ilma.

24. Allahumma inni a'udhu bika min sharri nafsi wa
min sharri kulli dabbatin anta akhidhun binasiyati-

ha, inna rabbi 'ala siratin mustaqim.

25. Ya Hayyu ya Qayyum! Birahmatika astaghithu wa min 'adhabika astajir. Aslih li sha'ni kullahu wa la takilni ila nafsi wa la illa ahadin min khalqika tarfata 'ayn.

26. Allahumma inni a'udhu bika min'al-hammi wal-haz-an, wa a'udhu bika min'al-'ajzi wal-kasal, wa a'udhu bika min'al-jubni wal-bukhl, wa a'udhu bika min ghalabat'id-dayni wa qahri'r-rijal.

27. Allahumma inni as'aluka'l-'afwa wal-'afiata wal mu'afat' ad-da'imata fi dini wa dunyaya wa ahli wa mali.

28. Allahumma'stur 'awrati wa amin raw'ati.

29. Allahumma'h fadhni min bayni yadayya wa min khalfi, wa 'an yamini wa 'an shimali wa min fawqi, wa a'udhu bi 'ad hamatika an ughtala min tahti.

30. Allahumma anta khalaqtani wa anta tahdini, wa anta tut'imuni wa anta tasqini, wa anta tumituni wa anta tuhyini.

31. Asbahna 'ala fitrat'il-Islam, wa 'ala kalimat'il-ikhlasi, wa 'ala dini nabiyyina Muhammadin, salla'Llahu 'alayhi wa alihi wa sallam', wa 'ala millati abina

Ibrahima, hanifan, Musliman, wa ma kana min'al-mushrikin.

32. Allahumma bika asbahna, wa bika amsayna, wa bika nahya, wa bika namutu, wa ilakya'n- nushur. [*In the evening: wa ilayk'al-masir.*]

33. Asbahna wa asbaha'l-mulku Iil'Llahi wal-hamdu lil'Llahi Rabbi'l-alamin. [*In the evening: amsayna wa amsa'l-mulku lil'Llahi...*]

34. Allahumma inni as'aluka khayra hadha'l-yawmi, fathahu, wa nasrahu, wa nurahu, wa barakatahu, wa hudah. [*In the evening: hadhihi'l-laylati, fathaha, wa nasraha, wa nuraha, wa barakataha, wa hudaha.*]

35. Allahumma inni as'aluka khayra hadha'l-yawmi wa khayra ma fih, wa a'udhu bika min sharri had-ha'l-yawmi wa sharri ma fih. [*In the evening: hadhi-hi'l-laylati wa khayra ma fiha wa a'udhu bika min sharri hadha'l-yawmmi wa sharri ma fiha, wa a'udhu bija min sharri hadihi'l-layalati wa sharri ma fiha.*]

36. Allahumma ma asbaha bi min ni'matin aw bi ahadin min khalqika faminka wahdaka, la sharika laka, falaka 'l-hamdu wa laka'sh-shukru 'ala dhalik. [*In the evening: Allahumma ma amsa…*]

37. Subhan'Allahi wa bi hamdih. [100 times]
38. Subhan'Allahi'l-'adhimi wa bi hamdih. [100 times]
39. Subhan'Allahi, wal-hamdu li'Llahi,, wa la ilaha
    illa'Llahu, wa'Llahu akbar. [100 times]
40. La ilaha illa'Llahu wahdahu la sharika lahu, la-
    hu'l-mulku wa lahu'l-hamdu, wa huwa 'ala kulli
    shay'in qadir. [100 times, mornings only]

الرَّاتب الشَّهير

Al-Ratib al-Shahir

INTRODUCTION

OF ALL THE litanies of Imam al-Haddad, the *Ratib* is the most famous. It has in fact acquired the title *Al-Ratib al-Shahir* or "The Famous Litany."

It came to the Imam by inspiration and was composed on the night of the twenty-seventh of Ramadan 1071 AH, *Laylat'ul-Qadr,* the Night of Destiny. The stimulus for its composition was a request by a student of the Imam, a man named Amir, from the Bani Sa'd, who lived in a village near Shibam. His purpose was to have a litany that would be a protection for all who recited it and would contain specific items pertaining to the beliefs of *Ahl al-Sunna wa'l Jama'a,* to counteract the effect of the Zaydi invasion of Hadramawt (the Zaydis being Shi'a but holding the Mu'tazilite belief that human beings create their own acts and that this is why people are held responsible for the evil they commit).

The orthodox position, on the other hand, is that humans intend their actions, but can only carry them out through Divine Power and Will, the secret of predestination lying beyond rational understanding and to be apprehended by direct spiritual vision in the life-to-come.

This is why Imam al-Haddad says in his *Ratib*: "In the name of God, all praise belongs to God. Both good and evil are by the will of God," which means that everything happens by God, for which He alone is to be praised, since good and evil are necessary components of life in this world, both being ordained by Divine Wisdom and Will.

The *Ratib* was first instituted in Amir's village by the Imam's permission, then at the Imam's mosque at al-Hawi in 1072 AH. It was recited in congregation after the Evening (*'Isha*) Prayer, its sunnas and invocations, except in Ramadan, when it was recited before *'Isha* to make room for the *Tarawih* prayers.

The Imam said that the *Ratib* protected the town where it was recited and helped people obtain from God all their requests. When he went on Hajj he instituted it in both Makkah and Madinah, and it continued to be recited there every night, near *Bab al-Safa* in Makkah and *Bab al-Rah-*

ma in Madinah, for years afterwards.

Sayyid Ahmad ibn Zayn al-Habashi said that he who would recite it with presence, reverence, certitude, and a strong intention, continuing with *la ilaha illa'Llah* to reach one thousand times (instead of the usual fifty) would not fail to have something of the Unseen unveiled before him.

Ideally the *Ratib* should be recited twice, after *fajr* and again after *'Isha*, but at least once after *'Isha* is acceptable. Al-Habib Ahmad Mashhur al-Haddad used to give special permission to recite the *Ratib* at other times as well as in times of need or stress.

Innumerable people in difficulty have recounted how recitation of the *Ratib* with specific intentions brought them prompt succour.

Imam Ahmad, son of al-Hasan, son of Abdallah al-Haddad, wrote a lengthy commentary of the *Ratib*, then bid his son, Imam Alawi ibn Ahmad, to expand on it. The latter's voluminous commentary was printed a few years ago in Singapore in Arabic. A *sayyid* of the Jamal al-Layl family wrote a brief commentary, and the famous scholar, Abdallah Ba-Sudan, a lengthier one. Both belong to the thirteenth century *Hijra* and were printed in Egypt.

Unlike the other litanies of Imam al-Haddad, which are meant for individual use, the *Ratib* is intended to be recited in a group. Each unit is recited thrice unless otherwise noted.

ARABIC & TRANSLATION

١) بِسْمِ اللَّهِ الرَّحْمَـٰنِ الرَّحِيمِ (١) ٱلْحَمْدُ لِلَّهِ رَبِّ ٱلْعَـٰلَمِينَ (٢) ٱلرَّحْمَـٰنِ ٱلرَّحِيمِ (٣) مَـٰلِكِ يَوْمِ ٱلدِّينِ (٤) إِيَّاكَ نَعْبُدُ وَإِيَّاكَ نَسْتَعِينُ (٥) ٱهْدِنَا ٱلصِّرَٰطَ ٱلْمُسْتَقِيمَ (٦) صِرَٰطَ ٱلَّذِينَ أَنْعَمْتَ عَلَيْهِمْ غَيْرِ ٱلْمَغْضُوبِ عَلَيْهِمْ وَلَا ٱلضَّآلِّينَ (٧)

In the Name of Allah, Most Merciful and Compassionate. All praise belongs to Allah, Lord of the Worlds. The Most Merciful, the Compassionate. Master of the Day of Reckoning. You only do we worship and to You only do we turn for help. Guide us to the straight path, the path of those whom You have favoured, not of those against whom You are wrathful, nor those who are astray. (I)

٢) ٱللَّهُ لَا إِلَـٰهَ إِلَّا هُوَ ٱلْحَيُّ ٱلْقَيُّومُ لَا تَأْخُذُهُ سِنَةٌ وَلَا نَوْمٌ لَّهُ مَا فِي ٱلسَّمَـٰوَٰتِ وَمَا فِي ٱلْأَرْضِ مَن ذَا ٱلَّذِي يَشْفَعُ عِندَهُ وَ إِلَّا

بِإِذْنِهِ ۚ يَعْلَمُ مَا بَيْنَ أَيْدِيهِمْ وَمَا خَلْفَهُمْ وَلَا يُحِيطُونَ بِشَيْءٍ مِّنْ عِلْمِهِ إِلَّا بِمَا شَاءَ ۚ وَسِعَ كُرْسِيُّهُ ٱلسَّمَٰوَٰتِ وَٱلْأَرْضَ ۖ وَلَا يَـُٔودُهُ حِفْظُهُمَا ۚ وَهُوَ ٱلْعَلِيُّ ٱلْعَظِيمُ (٢٥٥)

Allah, there is no god but He, the Living, the Sustainer; slumber overtakes Him not, nor sleep; to Him belongs everything that is in the heavens and the earth; who can intercede with Him save by His leave? He knows what is before them and what is behind them, and they comprehend nothing of His knowledge save such as He wills; His pedestal comprises the heavens and the earth, and it affects Him not to preserve them, He is the High, the Formidable. (2:225)

(3)　ءَامَنَ ٱلرَّسُولُ بِمَا أُنزِلَ إِلَيْهِ مِن رَّبِّهِ وَٱلْمُؤْمِنُونَ ۚ كُلٌّ ءَامَنَ بِٱللَّهِ وَمَلَٰئِكَتِهِ وَكُتُبِهِ وَرُسُلِهِ لَا نُفَرِّقُ بَيْنَ أَحَدٍ مِّن رُّسُلِهِ ۚ وَقَالُوا۟ سَمِعْنَا وَأَطَعْنَا ۖ غُفْرَانَكَ رَبَّنَا وَإِلَيْكَ ٱلْمَصِيرُ (٢٨٥) لَا يُكَلِّفُ ٱللَّهُ نَفْسًا إِلَّا وُسْعَهَا ۚ لَهَا مَا كَسَبَتْ وَعَلَيْهَا مَا ٱكْتَسَبَتْ ۗ رَبَّنَا لَا تُؤَاخِذْنَا إِن نَّسِينَا أَوْ أَخْطَأْنَا ۚ رَبَّنَا وَلَا تَحْمِلْ عَلَيْنَا إِصْرًا كَمَا حَمَلْتَهُ عَلَى ٱلَّذِينَ مِن قَبْلِنَا ۚ رَبَّنَا وَلَا تُحَمِّلْنَا مَا لَا طَاقَةَ لَنَا بِهِ ۖ وَٱعْفُ عَنَّا وَٱغْفِرْ لَنَا وَٱرْحَمْنَا ۚ أَنتَ مَوْلَٰنَا فَٱنصُرْنَا عَلَى ٱلْقَوْمِ ٱلْكَٰفِرِينَ (٢٨٦)

The Messenger believed in what was sent down to him from his Lord, and the believers; each one believed in Allah, His Angels, His Books, and His Messengers, we make no division between any of His Messengers; and they said: We hear and obey, Your forgiveness O our Lord, to You is the becoming! Allah charges no soul save to its capacity, to it what it has earned and against it what it has merited; our Lord, take us not to task if we forget or make mistakes; our Lord, charge us not with a burden such as You did lay upon those who were before us, our Lord, load not upon us that which we are unable to bear, and pardon us and forgive us and have mercy on us, You are our Patron, so help us against those who disbelieve. (2:285-286)

4) لَا إِلَـهَ إِلَّا اللَّـهُ وَحْـدَهُ لَا شَرِيكَ لَـهُ، لَـهُ الـمُلْكُ وَلَـهُ الحَمْـدُ، يُحْيِـي وَيُمِيـتُ وَهُـوَ عَـلَى كُلِّ شَيْءٍ قَدِيـر (ثلاثاً) *

There is no god save Allah, Alone; He has no partners. His is sovereignty and to Him belongs all praise. He gives life and He gives death, and over all things He has power.

5) سُبْحَانَ اللهِ، وَالحَمْدُ لِلَّهِ، وَلَا إِلَهَ إِلا اللهُ، وَاللَّهُ أَكْبَر (ثلاثاً) *

Transcendent is Allah, all praise belongs to Allah, there is no deity other than Allah, Allah is Greater.

6)   سُبْحَانَ اللهِ وَبِحَمْدِهِ، سُبْحَانَ اللهِ الْعَظِيمِ (ثلاثاً) *

Transcendent is Allah and by His praises! Transcendent is Allah the Formidable!

7)   رَبَّنَا اغْفِرْ لَنَا وَتُبْ عَلَيْنَا إِنَّكَ أَنْتَ التَّوَّابُ الرَّحِيمِ (ثلاثاً) *

Our Lord forgive us and relent toward us, for You are the Ever-Relenting, the Compassionate.

8)   اَللَّهُمَّ صَلِّ عَلَى مُحَمَّدٍ، اللَّهُمَّ صَلِّ عَلَيْهِ وَسَلِّمْ (ثلاثاً) *

O Allah, pray upon Muhammad! O Allah, pray upon him and give peace.

9)   أَعُوذُ بِكَلِمَاتِ اللهِ التَّامَّاتِ مِن شَرِّ مَا خَلَق (ثلاثاً) *

I take refuge in the complete words of Allah from the evil in what He has created.

(10)   بِسْـمِ اللهِ الَّـذِي لا يَـضُرُّ مَـعَ اسْـمِهِ شَـىْءٌ فِي الأَرْضِ وَلا فِي السَّـمَاءِ، وَهُـوَ السَّـمِيعُ العَلِيـمُ (ثلاثاً)*

In the Name of Allah, with Whose Name nothing on earth or in heaven can harm. He is the Hearer, the Knower.

(11)   رَضِينَا بِاللهِ رَبّاً، وَبِالإِسْلامِ دِينا، وَبِمُحَمَّدٍ نَبِيّا (ثلاثاً)*

We are content with Allah as Lord, with Islam as religion, and with Muhammad as Prophet.

(12)   بِسْمِ اللهِ، وَالحَمْدُ للهِ، والخَيْرُ والشَّرُّ بِمَشِيئَةِ اللهِ(ثلاثاً)*

In the Name of Allah, all praise belongs to Allah, both good and evil are by the will of Allah.

(13)   آمَنَّا بِاللهِ وَاليَوْمِ الآخِرِ، تُبْنَا إلى اللهِ بَاطِناً وَظَاهِرْ (ثلاثاً)*

We believe in Allah and the Last Day; we repent to Allah inwardly and outwardly.

(14)   يَا رَبَّنَا وَاعْفُ عَنَّا، وَامْحُ الَّذِي كَانَ مِنَّا (ثلاثاً) *

Our Lord, pardon us and erase whatever we may have committed.

(15)   يَاذَا الجَلالِ وَالإكْرَام، أَمِتْنَا عَلَى دِينِ الإسلام (سبعاً)*

O Possessor of Majesty and Generosity, make us die in the religion of Islam.

(16)   يَا قَوِيُّ يَا مَتِين، اِكْفِ شَرَّ الظَّالِمين (ثلاثاً)*

O Mighty! O Invincible! Keep away from us the evil of the unjust.

(17)   أَصْلَحَ اللهُ أُمُورَ المُسْلِمِين، صَرَفَ اللهُ شَرَّ المُؤْذِين (ثلاثاً)*

May Allah remedy the affairs of the Muslims; may Allah divert away from them the evil of evildoers.

(18)   يَا عَلِيُّ يَا كَبِير، يَا عَلِيمُ يَا قَدِير، يَاسَمِيعُ يَا بَصِير، يَا لَطِيفُ يَا خَبِير (ثلاثاً)*

O You Who are High, O You Who are Immense! O You
Who are Knowing, O You Who are Able! O You Who Hear,
O You Who See! O You Who are Gentle, O You Who are
Aware!

19) يَـا فَـارِجَ اَلهَـمّ، يَا كَاشِـفَ الغَـمّ، يَا مَـن لِعَبْـدِهِ يَغْفِـرُ
وَيَرْحَـم (ثلاثاً)*

O Reliever of grief! O Remover of distress! O You Who are
to His slave Forgiving and Compassionate!

20) أَسْتَغْفِرُ اَللهَ رَبَّ البَرَايَا، أَسْتَغْفِرُ اَللهَ مِنَ الخَطَايَا (أربعاً)*

I ask Allah for forgiveness, the Lord of all people, I ask Allah for forgiveness of all wrongdoing.

21) لا إلهَ إلاَّ اللّهُ (خمسين مرّةً وإن بَلَغها إلى ألفٍ كان حسناً)*

There is no deity other than Allah.

22) مُحَمَّـدٌ رَسُـولُ اَللّـه، صَـلَّى اَللّـهُ عَلَيـهِ وَآلِـهِ وَسَـلَّم، وَشَرَّفَ
وَكَـرَّم، وَمَجَّـدَ وَعَظَّـم، وَرَضِيَ اَللّـهُ عَـن أَهْـلِ بَيْتِـهِ الطَّيِّبِـينَ

الطَّاهِرِيـنَ، وَأَصْحَابِهِ الأَخْيَـارِ المُهْتَدِيـنَ، والتَّابِعِيـنَ لَهُـمْ بِإِحْسَـانٍ إلي يَـوْمِ الدِّيـنِ*

Muhammad is the Messenger of Allah, may Allah bless him and his family and grant them peace; may He honour, elevate, glorify, and magnify him. May He be well-pleased with his family, the good and pure, his Companions, the best of people, the rightly guided, and those who follow them with excellence till the Day of Reckoning.

23)   بِسْمِ اللَّهِ الرَّحْمَنِ الرَّحِيمِ

قُلْ هُوَ اللَّهُ أَحَدٌ (١) اللَّهُ الصَّمَدُ (٢) لَمْ يَـلِدْ وَلَمْ يُولَـدْ (٣) وَلَـمْ يَكُنْ لَـهُ كُفُواً أَحَـدٌ (٤) (ثلاثاً)

In the Name of Allah, the Most Merciful, the Compassionate. Say: He, Allah, is one. Allah is the eternally Besought. He has not begotten, nor been begotten, and equal to Him there is none. (112)

24)   بِسْمِ اللَّهِ الرَّحْمَنِ الرَّحِيمِ

قُلْ أَعُوذُ بِـرَبِّ الفَلَقِ (١) مِـنْ شَرِّ مَا خَلَـقَ (٢) وَمِـنْ شَرِّ غَاسِـقٍ إِذَا وَقَبَ (٣) وَمِـنْ شَرِّ النَّفَّـاثَـاتِ فِي الْعُقَدِ (٤) وَمِـنْ شَرِّ حَاسِـدٍ إِذَا حَسَـدَ (٥) (ثلاثاً)

In the Name of Allah, the Most Merciful, the Compassionate. Say: I take refuge with the Lord of the daybreak; from the evil of what He has created; from the evil of darkness when it gathers; from the evil of the women who blow on knots; and from the evil of an envier when he envies. (113)

(25) بِسْمِ اللَّهِ الرَّحْمَٰنِ الرَّحِيمِ

قُلْ أَعُوذُ بِرَبِّ ٱلنَّاسِ (١) مَلِكِ ٱلنَّاسِ (٢) إِلَٰهِ ٱلنَّاسِ (٣) مِن شَرِّ ٱلْوَسْوَاسِ ٱلْخَنَّاسِ (٤) ٱلَّذِي يُوَسْوِسُ فِي صُدُورِ ٱلنَّاسِ (٥) مِنَ ٱلْجِنَّةِ وَٱلنَّاسِ (٦) (ثلاثاً)

In the Name of Allah, the Most Merciful, the Compassionate. Say: I take refuge with the Lord of men; the King of men; the God of men; from the evil of the withdrawing whisperer; who whispers in the breasts of men; of jinn and men. (114)

(26) الفَاتِحَةُ إِلَى كَافَّةِ عِبَادِ اللَّهِ الصَّالِحِينَ، وَلِوَالِدِينَا، وَجَمِيعِ المُؤْمِنِينَ وَالـمُؤْمِنَاتِ وَالـمُسْلِمِينَ وَالـمُسْلِمَاتِ، أَنَّ اللَّهَ يَغْفِرُ لَهَمْ وَيَرْحَمُهُمْ، وَيَنْفَعُنَا بِأَسْرَارِهِمْ وَبَرَكَاتِهِمْ .... وَإِلَى حَضْرَةِ النَّبِيِّ مُحَمَّدٍ صَلَّى اللهُ عَلَيْهِ وَسَلَّمَ *

The Fatiha to all virtuous servants of Allah, our two parents, all male and female believers and all male and female Muslims, that Allah forgive them, have mercy on them, and give us benefit from their secrets and blessings.... Then one makes as much dua as one wants for oneself and all Muslims, then says: (And to the venerable Prophet Muhammad ﷺ). Once, then recite al-Fatiha once.

(27)   اللّهُـمَّ إنّـا نَسْـأَلُك رِضَـاكَ والجّنـة وَنَعـوذُ بِـكَ مِـن سَـخَطِكَ
والنّـار*

Allah, we ask You for Your good pleasure and the Garden and we seek Your protection from Your displeasure and the Fire!

TRANSLITERATION

1. BismiLlahi'r-Rahmani'r-Rahim. Al-hamdu li'Llahi Rab-
    bi'l-'alamin. Ar-Rahmani'r-Rahim. Maliki Yawmi'd-din.
    Iyyaka na'budu wa iyyaka nasta'in. Ihdina's-sirata'l-mus-
    taqim. Sirat'alladhina an'amta 'alayhim. Ghayri'l-maghdu-
    bi 'alayhim wa la'd-dallin. Amin! (1) [once]

2. Allahu La ilaha illa Huwa'l-Hayyu'l-Qayyum; la ta'khu-
    dhuhu sinatun wa la nawm; lahu ma fis'samawati wa ma
    fil-'ard; man dha'lladhi yashfa'u 'indahu illa bi'idhnih;
    ya'lamu ma bayna aydihim wa ma khalfahum wa la
    yuhituna bi shay'in min 'ilmihi illa bima sha'; wasi'a kur-
    siyyuhu's-samawati wal'arda wa la ya'uduhu hifd huhuma
    wa Huwa'l-'Aliyyu'l-Adhim. (2:255) [once]

3. Amana'r-rasulu bima unzila ilayhi min rabbihi wal-
    mu'minun; kullun amana biLlahi wa mala'ikatihi wa
    kutubuhi wa rusulih, la nufarriqu bayna ahadin min ru-

sulih wa qalu sami'na wa atan'na, ghufranaka rabbana wa
ilayka'l-masir. La yukallifu'Llahu nafsan illa wus'aha, laha
ma kasabat wa 'alayha ma'katsabt; rabbana la tu'akhidhna
in nasina aw akhta'na, rabbana wa la tahmil 'alayna isran
kama hamaltahu 'ala'l-ladhina min qablina, rabbana wa la
tuhammilna ma la taqata lana, wa'rhamna, anta mawlana
fan'surna 'ala'l-qawmi'l-kafirin. (2:285-286) [once]

4. La ilaha illa'Llahu wahdahu la sharika lah, lahu'l-mulku
wa lahu'l-hamd, yuhyi wa yumtiu wa huwa 'ala kulli
shay'in qadir.

5. Subhan'Allah, wal-hamdu li'Llah, wa la ilaha illa'Llah,
wa'Llahu akbar.

6. Subhan 'Allahi wa bihamdihi, Subhan 'Allahi'l-'Adhim.

7. Rabbana'ghafir lana wa tub 'alayna, innaka anta't-Tawwabu'r-Rahim.

8. Allahumma salli 'ala Muhammed, Allahumma salli 'alayhi
wa sallim.

9. A'udhu bi kalimati'l'Llahi't-tammati min sharri ma khalaq.

10. BismiLlahi'lladhi la yadurru ma'asmihi shay'un fi'l-ardi wa
la fi's-sama, wa huwa's-Sami'u'l-'Alim.

11. Radina biLlahi Rabban, wa bil'Islam dinan, wa bi Muhammadin nabiyya.

12. BismiLlah, wal-hamdu lil'Llah, wal-khayru wa'sh-sharru
    bi mashi'at'illah.

13. Amanna bil'Llahi wal-yawmi'l'akhir, tubna ila'Llahi bati-
    nan wa dhahir.

14. Ya Rabbana wa'fu 'anna, wa'mhu'lladhi kana minna.

15. Ya Dhal-Jalali wal'Ikram, amitna 'ala dini'l'Islam. [7 times]

16. Ya Qawiyyu ya Matin, ikfi sharra'dh-dhalimin.

17. Aslaha'Llahu umura'l-muslimin, sarafa'Llahu sharra'l
    mu'dhin.

18. Ya 'Aliyu ya Kabir, ya 'Alimu ya Qadir, ya Sami'u ya Basir,
    ya Latifu ya Khabir.

19. Ya Farija'l-hamm! Ya Kashifa'l-ghamm! Ya Man li'abdihi
    yaghfiru wa yarhamm!

20. Astaghfirul'Llaha Rabba'l-baraya, astaghfirul'Llaha min
    al-khataya. [4 times]

21. La ilaha illa'Llah. [50 or 1000 times]

22. Muhammadun Rasulu'Llahi, salla'Llahu 'alayhi wa alihi
    wa sallama, wa sharrafa wa karrama, wa majjada wa 'adh-
    dhama, wa radiya 'an ahli baytihi at - tayyibina' t- tahirin,
    wa ashabihi'l-akhyari'l-muhtadin, wat'tabi'ina lahum bi
    ihsanin ila yawmi'd-din. [once]

23. BismiLlahi'r'Rahmani'Rahim. Qul huwa'Llahu Ahad,

Allahu's Samad, lam yalid, wa lam yulad, wa lam yakun lahu kufuwan ahad.

24. Qul a'udhu birabbi'l-falaq; min sharri ma khalaq; wa min sharri ghasiqin idha waqab; wa min sharri'n-naffathati fil-'uqad; wa min sharri hasidin idha hasad.

25. Qul a'udhu birabbi'n-nas; maliki'n-nas; ilahi'n-nas; min sharri'l-waswasi'l-khannas; alladhi yuwaswisu fi suduri'n-nas; mi'nal-jinnati wa'n-nas.

26. Al-Fatiha ila kafati 'ibadi'Llahi's'salihin, waliwalidayni, wa jami'i'l'mu'minina wal-mu'minati wal-muslimina wal-muslimati, anna'Llaha yaghfiru lahum wayarhamuhum, wa yanfa'una bi asrarihim wa barakatihim... wa ila hadrat'an'nabiyyi Muhammadin salla'Llahu 'alayhi was sallam.

27. Allahumma inna nas'aluka ridaka wal-janna, wa na'udhu bika min sakhatika wan'nar.

COMMENTARY

I. Merits of *Surat al-Fatiha*

The Companion Abu Rafi' ibn al-Mu'alla ﷺ said: "As I was praying in the mosque, the Prophet ﷺ called me and I did not answer him, but I went to him thereafter and explained that I had been praying, whereupon he asked me whether or not God had not said: *Respond to God and to the Messenger when he calls you* (8:24), adding: *'Let me teach you the greatest sura in the Quran before you leave the mosque.'* He then took me by the hand, and when we were about to go out, I reminded him that he had said he would teach me the greatest sura in the Quran. He said: 'It is, *Al-hamdu li'Llahi Rabbi'l-'alamin [i.e. al-Fatiha]*; they are the seven oft-repeated verses [*al-sab' al-mathani*] and the Formidable Quran which was given to me."

Ibn Abbas ﷺ recounted that once Gabriel ﷺ was sitting with the Prophet 🌸 and heard a sound above him, at which he raised his head and said: "This is a gate opened in heaven today which has never been opened before." Then an angel descended through it and he continued: "This is an angel who has come down to earth, who has never come down before" The angel greeted them with salam, then said: "Rejoice in two lights given to you which were never given to any Prophet before you: *Fatihat'al-Kitab* and the last verses of *Surat al-Baqara*. No portion of them will you ever recite without being accorded it."

Abu Hurayra 🌸 related the following well-known hadith:

God—Exalted is He!—says: "I have divided the prayer [al-Fatiha] in two portions between Myself and My servant, and to My servant [I grant] what he asks. Half of it is Mine and half My servant's." When the servant says: "*All Praise belongs to God, Lord of all the Worlds,*" God says: "My servant praises Me!" When he says: "*The Most Merciful, the Compassionate,*" God says: "My servant lauds Me!" When he says: "*Master of the Day of Reckoning,*" God says: "My servant glorifies Me!" When he says: "*You only do we worship and to You only do we turn for help,*" God says: "This one is between Me and My servant, and My servant shall be granted his request!" And when he says: *"Guide us to the straight path, the path of those whom You have favoured, not of those against whom You are wrathful, nor those who are astray,"* God says: "This is for My servant and My servant shall be granted his request!"

The Prophet 🙵 once said to Ubayy ibn Ka'b 🙵 "By Him in whose Hand is my soul, nothing like it was revealed in the Torah, Gospel, Psalms, or the Furqan. It is the seven oft-repeated verses and the Formidable Quran which I have been given."

As for *"Amin!"* it essentially means, "Hear us, our Lord, and respond!" The Prophet 🙵 said: "When the Imam says, 'Amin!' repeat after him, for he whose 'Amin!' coincides with that of the angels, his sins are forgiven."

2. Merits of *Ayat al-Kursi*

The great Companion Ubayy ibn Ka'b 🙵 said that the Messenger of God 🙵, once asked Abu-l'Mundhir 🙵 "Do you know which verse of the Book of God that you have is the greatest?" Abu-l'Mundhir replied: "God and His Messenger know best!" He repeated his question until Abu-l'Mundhir said: "*God, there is no god but He, the Living, the Sustainer*"? Thereupon the Prophet ﷺ struck Abu-l'Mundhir on the breast, saying, out of happiness: "May knowledge be your delight, O Abu-l'Mundhir!"

When asked which sura of the Quran was greatest, the Prophet ﷺ answered: "*Qul huwa'Llahu Ahad*" (112). Then when asked which verse of the Quran was greatest, he answered: "*Allahu la ilaha illa Huwa'l-Hayyu'l-Qayyum*" (*Ayat'l-Kursi* 2:255). The same man then asked which verse he should be given to bring good to him and his people and the reply was: "The end of *Surat al-Baqara,* for it is one of the treasures of God's mercy from under His Throne, which He gave to His people, and there is no good in this world or the next that it does not include."

3. Merits of the last two verses of *Surat al-Baqara*

The Prophet ﷺ said: "Two thousand years before creating the heavens and the earth God inscribed a book, two verses of which He sent down that He concluded *Surat al-Baqara* with. The devil will not come near a house in which they are recited three nights."

The Prophet ﷺ said: "God concludes *Surat al-Baqara* with two verses which I have been given from His treasure under His Throne; so learn them and teach them to your womenfolk, for they are a blessing, a means to draw near and a prayer." The Prophet e said: "If anyone recites the last two verses of *Surat al-Baqara* at night they will avert harm from him."

4. Merits of the invocation

The Prophet ﷺ said: "He who says in the morning, *La ila-ha illa'Llahu wahdahu la sharika lah, lahu'l-mulki wa la-hu'l-hamd, yuhyi wa yumitu wa huwa 'ala kulli shay'in qadir*, his will be the equivalent of freeing ten slaves of the Children of Ishmael; ten good deeds will be recorded for him; ten bad ones erased; he will be raised ten degrees; and he will be protected from the Devil until nightfall. Should he say it in the evening he will receive the same until morning."

5. Merits of the invocation

The Prophet ﷺ said: "To say *Subhan'Allah, wal-hamdu*

li'Llah, wa la ilaha illa'Llah, wa'Llahu akbar is more pleasing to me than everything under the sun".

He also said: "The best of speech is *"Subhan'Allah, wal-hamdu li'Llah, wa la ilaha illa'Llah, wa 'Llahu akbar"*.

And he said: "I met Abraham on the night I was made to journey, and he said: 'O Muhammad! Convey my greetings to your community and inform them that the Garden has pleasing soil and sweet water and that it is made of fertile meadows and planted with *"Subhan'Allah, wal-hamdu lil'Llah, wa la ilaha illa'Llah, wa'Llahu akbar."'*

And he said: "In the Garden there are fertile meadows, plant them in abundance." His Companions ﷺ said: "O Messenger of God, how shall we plant them?" He replied: *"With Subhan'Allah, wal-hamdu li'Llah, wa la ilaha illa'Llah, wa'Llahu akbar."*

And he said: "God has selected four out of all words *"Subhan'Allah, wal-hamdu lil'Llah, wa la ilaha illa'Llah, wa'Llahu akbar.* He who says Subhan'Allah! twenty good deeds are written to his credit and twenty bad ones erased. To him who says, *Allahu akbar!* the same also happens. To him who says, *la ilaha illa'Llah!* the same also happens. To him who says of his own accord, *al-hamdu li'Llahi Rab-*

bi'l- alamin!, thirty good deeds are recorded and thirty bad ones erased."

6. Merits of the invocation

The Prophet ﷺ said: "Two words, light on the tongue, heavy in the scale, and dear to the Most Merciful: *Subhan Allahi wa bihamdihi, subhan Allahi'l-'Adhim.*" This is the last hadith in Bukhari's compilation. The meaning is: Transcendent is God beyond our ability to praise Him, therefore, we praise Him by His praises of Himself, since none knows Him truly but Himself. Transcendent is God, Formidable beyond conception; Great beyond words, utterly Incomparable.

7. Merits of the invocation

God says in the Quran: *Ask forgiveness of your Lord, then repent to Him...* (11:3). The order to ask for God's forgiveness is very frequently followed by an order to repent. As God says on the tongue of His Prophet Hud ﷺ: *"O my people, ask forgiveness of your Lord, then repent to Him, and He will send the skies pouring abundant rain, and He will increase you in strength unto your strength"* (11:52). This is because when one asks for forgiveness and is granted it, and then commits the same errors or sins again, he becomes as one who makes a mockery of Divine orders and prohibitions, thus deserving severe chastisement. But when one follows his request for forgiveness by repentance, then to the contrary, he rises in the sight of God and his evil deeds are converted in his book into good ones.

Repentance consists of regretting the wrong, one has committed; repairing it if it concerned another person's right; and forming a strong intention never to fall into the same error again. Even if, out of human weakness, one falls into the same error again, one should repeat the sequence of asking for forgiveness followed by repentance. When these are sincere, then even if one relapses a hundred times, God will forgive him a hundred times.

When repeating this invocation we should intend those errors which we are aware of and those which we might have committed while unaware or have forgotten.

Then we say: *Innaka anta't-Tawwabu'r-Rahim*—"You are the Ever-Relenting, the Compassionate." We call upon God by these attributes that He may accept our repentance and make it sound and permanent through His attribute *al-Tawwab* (the

Ever-Relenting), then grant us guidance, success in following the straight path, and paradise through His attribute *al-Rahim* (the Compassionate).

8. Merits of the prayer on the Prophet ﷺ

The Prophet ﷺ said: "Gabriel came to me and told me that my Lord says: 'Will it not please you, Muhammad, that none of your people will invoke a blessing on you without My blessing him ten times, and that none of your people will give you a greeting without My greeting him ten times?'"

The Prophet ﷺ also said: "He who invokes blessings on me once, God will bless him ten times, ten of his sins will be remitted, and he will be raised ten degrees." And he said: "The one who will be nearest to me on the Day of Resurrection will be the one who invoked most blessings on me."

9. Merits of the invocation

The Prophet ﷺ said: "He who says three times at nightfall, *A'udhu bi kalimati'l'Llahi't-tammati min sharri ma khalaq*, no harmful thing shall affect him that night."

10. Merits of the invocation:

The Prophet ﷺ said: "He who says: *BismiLlahi'lladhi la yadurru ma'asmihi shay'un fi'l-ardi wa la fi's-sama', wa huwa's-Sami'u'l-'Alim*, three times in the evening is safe from sudden afflictions till morning, and he who says it three times in the morning is safe from sudden afflictions till evening."

11. Merits of the invocation

The Prophet ﷺ said: "He who says every morning and evening, *Radina biLlahi Rabban, wa bil'Islami dinan, wa bi Muhammadin nabiyya*, certainly God will suffice him." In Imam Ahmad's Musnad, the same hadith is quoted with the addition that it is to be said thrice in the evening and thrice in the morning.

And the Prophet ﷺ said: "He who says in the morning, *Radina biLlahi Rabban, wa bil'Islami dinan, wa bi Muhammadin nabiyya*, I shall be responsible for taking his hand until I lead him into the Garden."

12. Merits of the invocation

"In the name of God" means we know that everything in

the universe happens by the Will of God, in His name, the name of the King, and nothing can happen that He has not willed. With BismiLlah everything begins.

"Praise belongs to God" means that all that happens in the universe happens according to the infinite mercy, wisdom, and grace of God. He is deserving of praise for everything in the universe, whether according to our perceptions it is good or evil, for both are components of the total Divine plan, which is ultimately good, because it is willed by the Supreme Good.

This is the article of faith that contradicts the beliefs of deviant sects. It is why just as every act is initiated with *BismiLlah* it is concluded with *al-hamdu lil'Llah*. Whatever begins by the name of God must be concluded with thanks and praises to Him.

13. Merits of the invocation

This is a reaffirmation of two of the articles of faith (belief in God and the Last Day), following upon the affirmation of Divine Decrees in the previous invocation. The implication of belief in God and the Last Day is that we are ever returning to Him, repenting to Him, and correcting both our inwards and outwards to conform to the pattern that will lead to security on the Last Day. Belief in God means acknowledging that our upright behaviour comes from Him and that He receives us when we err and repent. Belief in the Last Day implies acknowledging that we must conform to the rulings of *Shariah* to reach that Day in a hopeful state.

14. Merits of the invocation

Ya Rabbana: Calling upon the *Rabb* (Lord), who is the Affectionate Protector, looking after His dependents, supervising them leniently, and rescuing them when they stumble.

Wa'fu'anna: "Pardon us," do not punish us when we err. The difference between *pardon* and *forgiveness* is that to pardon is not to punish, while to forgive is not only not to punish, but also to conceal the error and protect from scandal. This is why the next request is: *wa'mhu'lladhi kana minna* "Erase whatever [wrong] we may have committed," erase it from our record and erase the evil consequences of it, whether inward in the heart, outward in the world, or later in the Hereafter.

15. Merits of the invocation

Divine Attributes are of two main kinds: attributes of Majesty and attributes of Beauty. Majesty is awesome, transcendent, implacable in justice and in exacting revenge, and overpowering. Beauty is mercy, gentleness, forgiveness, grace, and intimacy. Beyond both lies the ineffable Divine Essence.

To say: *Ya Dhal-Jalali wal'Ikram*! is to call upon God by both His attributes of rigour and mercy. The Prophet ﷺ once heard a man saying "*Ya Dhal-Jalali wal'Ikram*" He told him "You have been answered, so ask!"

In this prayer, the Imam is asking for his life to be concluded in the right way when the ultimate time comes, that is to say, to die a Muslim. We are all enjoined to ask God for a good conclusion to our lives (*husn al-khatima*), since the most excellent life if concluded wrongly will be of no avail. The weakest moment in one's life is the moment of death, and this is when one is most vulnerable to the action of the Devil. If one's faith is weak due to deviant beliefs, illusory attachments, or sins, he may well succumb to the satanic onslaught of the last moment and die a disbeliever. But he whose faith is strong, whose main attachment is to God and His Prophet ﷺ is, and whose behaviour is, in the main, in conformity with *Shariah*, he will receive the support of the angels and men of God and will be able to resist the Devil's insidious attacks.

The Lord of Majesty is He who has decreed death for all creatures, set a time for each, and causes them to die. None can give death but He. He is also the One who created Satan. He is also the Lord of Generosity who grants His servants the graces of faith and good behaviour, who casts into their hearts the love of Him, His Prophets and saints, and grants them firmness and support at the time of death. This is our God who encompasses the most excellent of attributes.

The meaning of the prayer is thus: O You who created men and the means for their salvation and perdition, who made death ineluctable and followed by either perpetual bliss or torment, we acknowledge Your sovereignty, power, and justice, but we throw ourselves into the ocean of Your mercy, that You may save us from the evil ending and the Fire and grant us the good ending and the Garden. This is equivalent to the Prophetic prayer: "I seek protection in Your good pleasure from Your wrath!"

16. Merits of the invocation

Ya Qawiy (O Strong!): O You whose action in His creation is strong, whose power is irresistible!

Ya Mattin (O Invincible!): O You who are invincible in Yourself, unaffected by any of Your creation!

Both of these are attributes of Majesty, and they are used to seek protection against the evil of the unjust, the iniquitous, and the tyrants, who are manifestations of other attributes of Majesty; for He guides whom He will and He leads whom He will astray. He elevates some men above others and allows them to oppress them. He unleashes the tyrants to punish the people.

Ikfi sharra'z- zalimin! God's attribute *al-Kafi* or He who suffices. In this context it is He who suffices as protection against the evil of oppressors. Here again we are seeking the protection of a Divine Attribute of Mercy against the manifestations of rigour.

17. Merits of the invocation

The Prophet ﷺ said: "No Muslim servant shall pray for his brother, unknown to him, without the responsible angel saying: 'And as much for you!'" And the Prophet ﷺ said: "The prayer of a Muslim for his brother, unknown to him, is [always] answered. There is an angel standing near his head, whenever he prays for his brother a beneficent prayer, the angel says: *"Amin*! And as much for you!'"

Whenever we make a prayer we should remember all the Muslim community, good ones and bad ones; Sunni, Shi'a, everyone. Whatever our differences, we are part of the organic whole that is the Muhammadan Nation, and if the Prophet ﷺ cares for us, we should also care.

18. Merits of the invocation

Al-Ali (the Most High): Imam al-Ghazali ﷺ says, "The Most High is the One above whose rank there is no rank, and all ranks are inferior to Him."[1] He also says: "Objects [are] divided into causes and effects, so that the cause is above the effect—above in rank; yet only the Cause of Causes is above absolutely."[2] That is every cause is higher than its effect, which applies to chains of causes and effects. All causes in the universe are secondary causes: there is one First Cause with nothing above or before it, and that is God. He is, therefore, High in absolute terms. Then Imam al-Ghazali goes on to point out that God uses examples from the material world to indicate higher realities and that when people are dim enough to take these literally, absurdities arise, such as assigning a spatial location to the Infinite. He gives an example of how one of those who take things literally would be discomfited if told that two distinguished individuals, one being superior in rank to the other, were sitting next to each other in an assembly. "He might say 'this one sits above that one,' knowing that he only sits at his side. For he would only be seated above him if he were seated on his head…"[3] This is how one should understand how God is "on" His throne.

Al-Kabir (the Immense): This is as saying "the Infinite," for He is Great in an absolute sense and nothing can he compared to His greatness. This is why it is said in a hadith that the earth and terrestrial heaven are as a ring cast into the wilderness compared with the heaven above it. And the heaven above it is as a ring in the wilderness compared with the one above it. And so on, with every heaven until the Pedestal, within which the seven heavens and seven earths are as a ring in the wilderness. The Pedestal stands in the same relationship to the Throne. But the Throne, mighty beyond conception, stands as naught in the Divine presence. For it is finite and the finite is strictly naught before the Infinite. Allahu Akbar!

Al-'Alim (the Omniscient): God is He who knows everything, simultaneously, in the most minute detail and ultimate clarity. Any creature of His may know things only to the extent that He bestows upon it of His knowledge. His knowledge does not arise from knowing things; rather, things arise as a consequence of His eternal knowledge of them.

Al-Qadir (the Able): God is He who is capable of carrying out whatever He wills in exactly the way that He wills it. This attribute is mentioned frequently in the Quran: He has power over all things [or all acts].

Al-Sami' (The Hearer or the All-Hearing): He is one who hears everything in the universe that is audible. He hears all sounds, those that are perceptible to human ears or to any other mode of hearing, simultaneously and distinctly, no sound impinging upon the others. He also hears the whisperings in the breasts and the prayers in the hearts. The realm of hearing that He manifests in creation allows all creatures that hear to hear, each according to the mode He allows them.

Al-Basir (the All-Seeing): One who sees everything simultaneously and distinctly—what is visible to creatures and what is not. The realm of vision that He manifests in creation allows every creature endowed with vision to see, each according to the mode specific to it.

Al-Latif (the Gentle, the Subtle, the Benevolent): God is He who executes His decrees in a gentle manner, wraps affliction in a cloak of mercy, attenuates punishments, relieves stresses, and grants ease within hardship.

Al-Khabir (the Aware): He is the Knower whose knowledge arises from knowing things from the inside; He knows inwards and outwards as part of His omniscience.

The invocation begins with praising God with His attributes of transcendence, then His knowledge and ability, as if one were saying: "O You who are beyond conception and beyond comparison, You who are All-Knowing and All-Powerful, thus Able to do all things." Then we call upon His attributes of hearing and vision, as if to say: "You hear our pleas! You see our states!" Then we call upon His gentle responsiveness and awareness, as if to say: "Treat us with mercy. You who are Aware of our feelings and innermost thoughts, give us what we want, remove our hardships, gladden our hearts!"

19 & 20. Merits of the invocation

The Prophet ﷺ said: "When a servant commits a sin, a spot is inscribed on his heart. Should he then refrain and ask for forgiveness, it is removed. When he repeats it a larger one appears, until his heart is enveloped by it. This is as God the Exalted says: Nay! But the evil they earned covered their hearts (83:14).

The Prophet ﷺ also said: "Hearts suffer from rust as the rust of copper; the polish of it is asking forgiveness." And he stated: "Iblis said: 'By Your Might! I shall not cease to tempt Your servants as long as their spirits remain in their bodies!' [God] said: 'By My Might and Majesty! I shall not cease to forgive them as long as they ask Me forgiveness!'" God says in a hadith *Qudsi*, "O My servants! You commit errors night and day. It is I who forgives all sins, so ask Me for forgiveness and I shall forgive you!"

21. Merits of La ilaha illa'Llah

Habib Ahmad Mashhur al-Haddad ﷺ wrote in his book *Key to the Garden*, which he devoted fully to an explanation and commentary on this noble phrase:

La ilaha illa'Llah: A phrase sublime in its meaning,

brief in its construction, vast in its effect, noble in its rank, brilliant in its light, and unique in its merit. It comprises four words upon which the Faith is founded and the *qibla* set. This is the phrase that was given in every Book sent down by God to every one of His noble Messengers, and through which one is rescued from the infernal fires and wins eternal happiness in the Gardens. God the Exalted has said: *Know that there is no god but God! (47:19); I am God, there is no god but Me, so worship Me! (20:14)*; God, there is no god but He, the Living, the Sustainer *(2:255)*; *God, there is no god but He, to Him belong the Most Beautiful Names (20:8); and We sent no Messenger before you without revealing to him: "There is no God but Me, so worship Me" (21:25).*

Through sound belief and certainty in its meaning, and by submission to it, one attains to faith or *iman*. By uttering it with sincerity, and truly acting in accordance with it, *Islam* results. By joining sound belief with submission to its authority there dawns in the heart the reality of excellence or *ihsan*.

The Phrase of *Tawhid* is also called the "Phrase of the Testimony," and of "Sincerity," "Reality," "Truth," "the Pledge," "Faith," "Piety," the "Good Word," the "Abiding Word," "God's Most Exalted Word," the "Word of Intercession," the "Price of the Garden," and the "Key to the Garden."

It is that with which a man first enters Islam, and the last thing he leaves the world with—to the Garden and eternal bliss. As the hadith says: "Whoever has for his last words in this life *La ilaha illa'Llah* shall enter the Garden." It is the first obligation, and also the last. Whoever says it with certainty and dies while holding fast to it shall have the joy of entering the Garden, as this hadith states. But whoever rejects it with arrogance, either by denial or by ascribing associates to God, shall enter the Fire, and there is no worse abode.

Those who arrogantly refrain from worshipping Me shall enter Hell subjugated (40:60); As for those who were scornful and arrogant, He will give them a pain-

ful torment, and they shall find no protecting friend or helper against God (4:173); God has forbidden the Garden to the one who ascribes partners to God, and his abode is the Fire (5:72.).

La ilaha illa'Llah means that God alone is worthy of worship. *Allah* is the noun which denotes the Holiest Essence, the Necessary Existent, who is possessed of all the attributes of perfection and majesty, is beyond contingency, beyond having associates or peers, beyond resembling anything, and beyond any attribute or state which does not befit His Glory and Magnitude. For He is the Unique Divinity, the One, the Self-Sufficient, who neither begets nor is begotten, who has no likeness. There is no god but Him, Transcendent is He. Nothing shares in His Essence, Attributes, or Actions; to Him belong Sovereignty and all praise, and He has power over all things.[4]

He also writes in the chapter entitled: "The Effects of *Tawhid* and of Its Noble Phrase":

The Two Testimonies are powerfully effective in refining the self, creating rectitude of character, and reinforcing social ties. The Testimony of *La ilaha illa 'Llah* liberates the mind from illusions, and purifies souls from the filth of idolatry, so that they rise up from the mire of their devotion to other than God (Exalted is He!) and from the debasement which inheres in worshipping idols, animals, and men. Hearts are united by it in the adoration of the one God, and faces are united in orienting themselves to the same *qibla*. *Tawhid* has a beneficial effect in uniting the hearts of the human race and making them work together for the common good and for the success of all. The Testimony of *Muhammadun rasulu'Llah* and belief in his Message and in his Upright Book strengthen morality, reform souls, and set an excellent example to be followed in all situations.

These two utterances are the believer's treasure and capital, the source of his happiness in this life and in the next: for those who behave strictly in accordance with them and draw light from their radiance in that which is necessary concerning *Tawhid* and attachment

to the Holiest Presence [*al-Janab al-Aqdas*], exposing
themselves to His spiritual gifts [*waridat imdadatih*],
and setting themselves in the way of the breaths of
reunion and the gifts of nearness; and that which is
necessary concerning following the Noblest Messenger, the Firmest Handhold [*al-'Urawat al-Wuthqa*],
the Excellent Example, in every religious and worldly transaction, for the goodness of one's daily life and
one's abode in the Afterlife, of the heart and the body,
the individual and the community. Around the pivot
of these Two Testimonies revolves the well-being of
the human race in both abodes.

Know that this noble phrase has two halves. First,
there is a negation, la ilaha ["there is no deity"], and
second there is an affirmation, *illa'Allah* ["except
God"]. When the negation is enounced, followed by
the affirmation, this signifies that a Muslim has acknowledged and established *Tawhid* in his heart by
means of this noble phrase, which is incompatible
with, and negates, the "Greater Idolatry" [*al-shirk
al-akbar*] the presence of which invalidates the foun-

dations of faith. *Tawhid* is strengthened by repeating it with the heart and the tongue. The Prophet ﷺ said "Renew your faith with *La ilaha illa'Llah*" It is also incompatible with, and negates, the "Lesser Idolatry," namely ostentation in worship, the desire to gain eminence and power over others, and all other actions in which one pays attention to with regard to others, desiring their praise and respect, and hoping for status in their eyes. The Prophet ﷺ said, "Idolatry in my nation is more imperceptible than the footfalls of ants." This Lesser Idolatry does not invalidate the foundations of faith, upon which one's salvation depends, but renders it defective. *La ilaha illa'Llah* destroys both the Greater and the Lesser Idolatry in whoever utters it with sincere faith and acts accordingly. The fact that *La ilaha* comes first means that the heart is cleared of these concealed things and these impurities. The subsequent affirmation of *illa'Llah* adorns and fills up the heart with the lights of *Tawhid* and faith. It is therefore not surprising that holding fast to, and repeating, this invocation brings about the purification of the heart, its cleansing from blemishes, and its illumination. Good deeds are reckoned in accordance with the number of repetitions of the invocation, each *La ilaha illa'Llah* being counted as one, while their reward is tenfold or multiplied many more times. If the person engaged in the Remembrance of God bears in mind that *La ilaha illa 'Llah* also a verse of the Quran and makes the intention to recite from the Quran together with making invocation, he gains the reward for Quranic recitation also.

A subtle indication [*ishara*] lies in the fact that the letters of the Testimony all arise from the depths of the body, and none of them are formed by the lips, which points to the fact that these should proceed from the purest inward part, which is the heart, and not from the lips. Also, none of the letters have dots, and this is an allusion to freedom from worshipping anything besides God.

La ilaha illa'Llah Muhammadun rasaulu'Llah consists of seven words. A man has seven members, and the Fire has seven doors, and each of the seven words closes one of the seven doors against one of the seven members.[3]

And Imam Abdallah al-Haddad 🕮 writes in Gifts for the Seeker under the section: *"La ilaha illa'Llah* as a formula for *dhikr"*:

> You should know that this phrase is the most comprehensive and profitable of all invocations; the nearest to bringing about the Opening and illumining of the heart with the light of God. It is also the most suitable of invocations for all people, since it includes the meanings of all other invocations, such as al-*hamdu li'Llah*, Subhan Allah, and so on. Each believer should, therefore, make it his inseparable *wird*, his constant *dhikr*, without, however, abandoning the other invocations, of each of which he should have a *wird*.

> Every human being is either a traveller, an arriver, or a non-traveller, and all three should hold unceasingly to this invocation. Travellers and non-travellers, since they perceive objects and attribute to them an existence of their own—something which may lead

to subtle forms of hidden *shirk*—can only expel these from their souls by constantly repeating this phrase. As for the man who has arrived, this invocation is again the most appropriate for him, because although he perceives things by God, and unceasingly summons them to Him, he is not entirely free from perceiving his own self from time to time, and from reprehensible thoughts unworthy of his rank. It has been handed down to us that Abu Bakr al-Siddiq ﷺ used to insert this phrase into his conversation: he would utter a few words, say, *La ilaha illa'Llah* and then resume what he was saying. This pertains to the Station of Subsistence [*Baqa*] which follows that of Extinction [*Fana'*]. As we said earlier, there is no invocation more appropriate for a man to constantly use than this; however, when the traveller reaches the initial stages of extinction, and is liberated from perceiving any of the worlds [as autonomous], then the most appropriate thing for him at that time is to keep to the name of Allah. This is what the people of gnosis have advised.

All the above is from the point of view of choosing

the best and most appropriate alternative, for otherwise all the invocations are paths leading to God. The shaykhs ﷺ have many methods of uttering this honourable Phrase, whether aloud or silently, and have set conditions which the invoker who would expose himself to the Divine effulgence and the Lordly Opening needs to fulfil. These are explained in those of their treatises which deal with them specifically, where they can he found by whoever wishes to tread the path of such men. It is best that those who are able to find in their time a shaykh of authority should receive these from him directly, since books are a last resort for those who are unable to find [such a teacher]; and what a difference there is between a man who receives the Path from a gnostic of authority who will take him to God, and one who only picks it up from a book!

God guides to what is right. To Him is the return, and success is from Him and in His Hand.

22. Merits of the invocation

The completion of the testimony of faith, *La ilaha illa'Llah* is *Muhammadun rasaulu'Llah*, Muhammad is the Messenger of God. The Prophet ﷺ said: "He who testifies that there is no god but God and that Muhammad is the Messenger of God, God forbids the Fire to him." The completion of the second testimony is *salla'Llahu 'alayhi wa sallam*, "may God send down His blessings and peace upon him." These prayers are embellished by two more things: further prayers to honour, ennoble, glorify, and magnify him, and also the inclusion of his household (his wives, children, and all his descendants), his Companions, and all those who follow them with excellence till the Last Day.

23. Merits of Surat *al-Ikhlas*

The Prophet ﷺ stated on more than one occasion that *Surat al-Ikhlas* was worth one third of the Quran. One of the Companions leading an expedition, always ended his Quranic recitations during the ritual Prayers with this *Sura*. This was mentioned to the Prophet ﷺ on their return, and he bid them to ask him why he did so. He replied: "Because it is the attribute of the All-Merciful

and I love to recite it." On hearing this, the Prophet &
said: "Tell him that God loves him."

Upon hearing a man recite *Surat al-Ikhlas,* the Prophet &
stated: "It has become incumbent!" Abu Hurayra & asked
the prophet & what had become incumbent, and the
prophet & replied that it was the Garden.

24 & 25. Merits of the *Mu'awwidhatyn*

The prophet & said: "what wondrous verses have been
revealed tonight! The like of them has never been seen.
They are: *Qul a'udhu birabbi'l-falaq and Qul a'udhu birabbi'n-nas,"* that is, the final two *Suras* of the Quran.

Aisha & said that every night when the prophet &
went to his bed, he joined his hands and breathed into
them, reciting: *Qul Huwa'Llahu Ahad, Qul a'udhu birabbi'll-falaq, and Qul a'udhu birabbi'n-nas* (112-113, and 114).
Then he would wipe as much of his body as he could with
his hands, beginning with his head, his face, and the front
of his body, doing that three times.

Once as the prophet & and some of his companions &
were travelling in the desert, not far from al-Abwa' where
the Prophet's mother is buried, they were enveloped by

wind and intense darkness. Whereupon the Prophet ﷺ began to recite, *Qul a'udu birabbi'l-falaaq* and *Qul a'udhu birabbi'n-nas.* He then turned to 'Uqba ibn Amir ﷺ, who was with him, and said: "Use them 'Uqba when seeking refuge in God, for there is nothing comparable to them toward that purpose."

Another Companion recounted how they went out on a dark, rainy night looking for the Prophet ﷺ. When they caught up with him, he told him: "Say!" The Companion asked him what he was to say. He replied: "Say, *Qul Huwa'Llahu Ahad* and the *Mu'awwidhatayn* three times morning and evening; they will serve you for every purpose."

To clarify the meanings of some of the expressions, the "women who blow on knots" are the sorceresses and the "envier" is he who gives the "evil eye," both being kinds of injurious behaviour mediated by the subtle world. The "withdrawing whisperer" is the devil. A hadith states: "The Devil's trunk rests on the Son of Adam's heart; when he remembers God, he withdraws, when he forgets, he gobbles his heart."

26. Merits of the invocation

The Prophet ﷺ said: "When someone asks God for the
Garden three times, the Garden says: 'O God! Make him
enter the Garden; and when someone asks protection from
the Fire three times, the Fire says: 'O God! Protect him
from the Fire!'

NOTES

1.   Imam al-Ghazali, The Ninety-Nine Beautiful Names of God, trans.
     David B. Burrel and Nazih Daher (Cambridge: Islamic Texts Society,
     1992), 102.

2.   Ibid., 104.

3.   Ibid., 105.

4.   Habib Ahmad Mashhur al-Haddad, Key to the Garden, second
     revised edition, translated by Mostafa al-Badawi (Claritas Books),
     25,26

5.   Ibid., 28-30

6.   Imam Abdallah al-Haddad, Gifts for the Seeker, trans. Mostafa
     al-Badawi (London: The Quilliam Press, 1992), 18-19.

ARABIC APPENDIX I:
Al-Wird al-Latif

الورد اللَّطيف

بِسْمِ اللَّهِ الرَّحْمَٰنِ الرَّحِيمِ

قُلْ هُوَ ٱللَّهُ أَحَدٌ (١) ٱللَّهُ ٱلصَّمَدُ (٢) لَمْ يَلِدْ وَلَمْ يُولَدْ (٣) وَلَمْ يَكُن لَّهُ كُفُواً أَحَدُۢ (٤) (ثلاثاً)

بِسْمِ اللَّهِ الرَّحْمَٰنِ الرَّحِيمِ

قُلْ أَعُوذُ بِرَبِّ ٱلْفَلَقِ (١) مِن شَرِّ مَا خَلَقَ (٢) وَمِن شَرِّ غَاسِقٍ إِذَا وَقَبَ (٣) وَمِن شَرِّ ٱلنَّفَّٰثَٰتِ فِي ٱلْعُقَدِ (٤) وَمِن شَرِّ حَاسِدٍ إِذَا حَسَدَ (٥) (ثلاثاً)

بِسْمِ اللَّهِ الرَّحْمَٰنِ الرَّحِيمِ

قُلْ أَعُوذُ بِرَبِّ ٱلنَّاسِ (١) مَلِكِ ٱلنَّاسِ (٢) إِلَٰهِ ٱلنَّاسِ (٣) مِن شَرِّ ٱلْوَسْوَاسِ ٱلْخَنَّاسِ (٤) ٱلَّذِي يُوَسْوِسُ فِي صُدُورِ ٱلنَّاسِ (٥) مِنَ ٱلْجِنَّةِ وَٱلنَّاسِ (٦) (ثلاثاً)

رَّبِّ أَعُوذُ بِكَ مِنْ هَمَزَاتِ ٱلشَّيَاطِينِ (٩٧) وَأَعُوذُ بِكَ رَبِّ أَن يَحْضُرُونِ (٩٨) (ثلاثاً)

أَفَحَسِبْتُمْ أَنَّمَا خَلَقْنَاكُمْ عَبَثاً وَأَنَّكُمْ إِلَيْنَا لَا تُرْجَعُونَ (١١٥) فَتَعَالَى ٱللَّهُ ٱلْمَلِكُ ٱلْحَقُّ لَا إِلَٰهَ إِلَّا هُوَ رَبُّ ٱلْعَرْشِ ٱلْكَرِيمِ (١١٦) وَمَن يَدْعُ مَعَ ٱللَّهِ إِلَٰهاً ءَاخَرَ لَا بُرْهَٰنَ لَهُ بِهِ فَإِنَّمَا حِسَابُهُ عِندَ رَبِّهِ إِنَّهُ لَا يُفْلِحُ ٱلْكَافِرُونَ (١١٧) وَقُل رَّبِّ ٱغْفِرْ وَٱرْحَمْ وَأَنتَ خَيْرُ ٱلرَّاحِمِينَ (١١٨)

فَسُبْحَانَ ٱللَّهِ حِينَ تُمْسُونَ وَحِينَ تُصْبِحُونَ (١٧) وَلَهُ ٱلْحَمْدُ فِى ٱلسَّمَٰوَٰتِ وَٱلْأَرْضِ وَعَشِيّاً وَحِينَ تُظْهِرُونَ (١٨) يُخْرِجُ ٱلْحَىَّ مِنَ ٱلْمَيِّتِ وَيُخْرِجُ ٱلْمَيِّتَ مِنَ ٱلْحَىِّ وَيُحْىِ ٱلْأَرْضَ بَعْدَ مَوْتِهَا وَكَذَٰلِكَ تُخْرَجُونَ (١٩)

أَعُوذُ بِاللهِ السَّمِيعِ الْعَلِيمِ مِنَ الشَّيْطَانِ الرَّجِيمِ (ثلاثاً)*

لَوْ أَنزَلْنَا هَٰذَا ٱلْقُرْءَانَ عَلَىٰ جَبَلٍ لَّرَأَيْتَهُ خَاشِعاً مُّتَصَدِّعاً مِّنْ خَشْيَةِ ٱللَّهِ وَتِلْكَ ٱلْأَمْثَٰلُ نَضْرِبُهَا لِلنَّاسِ لَعَلَّهُمْ يَتَفَكَّرُونَ (٢١) هُوَ ٱللَّهُ ٱلَّذِى لَآ إِلَٰهَ إِلَّا هُوَ عَٰلِمُ ٱلْغَيْبِ وَٱلشَّهَٰدَةِ هُوَ ٱلرَّحْمَٰنُ ٱلرَّحِيمُ (٢٢) هُوَ ٱللَّهُ ٱلَّذِى لَآ إِلَٰهَ إِلَّا هُوَ ٱلْمَلِكُ ٱلْقُدُّوسُ ٱلسَّلَٰمُ ٱلْمُؤْمِنُ ٱلْمُهَيْمِنُ ٱلْعَزِيزُ ٱلْجَبَّارُ ٱلْمُتَكَبِّرُ سُبْحَٰنَ ٱللَّهِ عَمَّا يُشْرِكُونَ (٢٣) هُوَ ٱللَّهُ ٱلْخَٰلِقُ ٱلْبَارِئُ ٱلْمُصَوِّرُ لَهُ ٱلْأَسْمَآءُ ٱلْحُسْنَىٰ يُسَبِّحُ لَهُ مَا

فِى ٱلسَّمُوتِ وَٱلْأَرْضِ وَهُوَ ٱلْعَزِيزُ ٱلْحَكِيمُ (٢٤)

سَلَـٰمٌ عَلَىٰ نُوحٍ فِى ٱلْعَـٰلَمِينَ (٧٩) إِنَّا كَذَٰلِكَ نَجْزِى ٱلْمُحْسِنِينَ (٨٠) إِنَّهُ مِنْ عِبَادِنَا ٱلْمُؤْمِنِينَ (٨١)

أَعُوذُ بِكَلِمَاتِ اللّٰهِ التَّامَّاتِ مِنْ شَرِّ مَا خَلَقَ (ثَلاثاً) * بِسم اللّٰهِ الَّذِي لا يَضُرُّ مَعَ اسْمِـهِ شَيْءٌ فِي الْأَرْضِ ولا فِي السَّمَاءِ، وَهُوَ السَّمِيعُ الْعَلِيم (ثَلاثاً) * اللّٰهُمَّ إِنِّي أَصْبَحْتُ مِنْكَ فِي نِعْمَةٍ وَعَافِيَةٍ وَسِتْرٍ، فَأَتِـمَّ نِعْمَتَكَ عَلَيَّ وَعَافِيَتَكَ وَسِتْرَكَ فِي الدُّنْيَا وَالآخِرَةِ (ثَلاثاً) * اللّٰهُمَّ إِنِّي أَصْبَحْتُ أُشْـهِدُكَ، وَأُشْـهِدُ حَمَلَةَ عَرْشِكَ، وَمَلائِكَتَكَ، وَجَمِيعَ خَلْقِكَ، أَنَّكَ أَنْتَ اللّٰهُ، لا إِلٰهَ إِلا أَنْتَ، وَحْدَكَ لا شَرِيكَ لَكَ، وَأَنَّ مُحَمَّداً عَبْدُكَ وَرَسُولُـكَ (أَربَعاً) * الْحَمْدُ للّٰهِ رَبِّ ٱلْعَالَمِين، حَمْداً يُـوَافِي نِعَمَـهُ وَيُكَافِئُ مَزِيدَهُ (ثَلاثاً) * آمَنْـتُ بِاللّٰهِ الْعَظِيمِ، وَكَفَرْتُ بِالْجِبْتِ وَالطَّاغُوت، وَاسْتَمْسَكْتُ بِالْعُرْوَةِ الْوُثْقَى، لَا انْفِصَامَ لَهَا، وَاللّٰهُ سَمِيعٌ عَلِيم (ثَلاثاً) * رَضِيتُ بِاللّٰهِ رَبّاً، وَبِالإِسْلام دِيناً، وَبِسَيِّدِنَا مُحَمَّد صَلَّى اللّٰهُ عَلَيْهِ وَسَلَّمَ، نَبِيّاً وَرَسُولاً (ثَلاثاً) * حَسْـبِيَ اللّٰهُ لا إِلٰهَ إِلّا هُـوَ، عَلَيْهِ تَوَكَّـلْتُ، وَهُـوَ رَبُّ الْعَرْشِ الْعَظِيم (سَبْعاً) * اللّٰهُمَّ صَلِّ عَلى سَيِّدِنَا مُحَمَّد وَآلِه وَصَحْبِـه وَسَلِّم (عَشْراً) * اللّٰهُمَّ إِنِّي أَسْأَلُكَ مِنْ فَجْأَةِ الْخَيـر، وَأَعُوذُ بِكَ مِـنْ فَجْأَةِ الشَّـرِّ * اللّٰهُمَّ أَنْتَ رَبِّي، لا إِلٰه إِلا أَنت خَلَقْتَنِي وَأَنَا عَبْدُك، وَأَنَا عَلَى عَهْدِكَ وَوَعْدِكَ مَا اسْتَطَعْتُ، أَعُوذُ بِكَ مِـنْ شَرِّ مَا صَنَعْت، أَبُوءُ لَكَ بِنِعْمَتِكَ عَلَيَّ وَأَبُوءُ بِذَنْبِي، فَاغْفِـرْلِي، فَإِنَّـهُ لا يَغْفِـرُ الذُّنُوبَ إِلا أَنت * اللّٰهُمَّ أَنْتَ رَبِّي لَا إِلٰهَ إِلّا

أنـت، عَلَيـكَ تَوَكَّلـتُ، وَأَنـتَ رَبُّ الْعَـرْشِ الْعَظِيـمِ * مَا شَـاءَ اللهُ كَانَ،
وَمَـا لَـمْ يَشَـأْ لَـمْ يَكُـنْ، ولا حَـوْلَ وَلا قُـوَّةَ إِلّا بِاللهِ الْعَلِـيِّ الْعَظِيـمِ *
أَعْلَـمُ أَنَّ اللهَ عَلَى كُلِّ شَيْءٍ قَدِيرٌ، وَأَنَّ اللهَ قَدْ أَحَاطَ بِكُلِّ شَيْءٍ عِلْما
* اللّهُـمَّ إِنِّي أَعُـوذُ بِـكَ مِـنْ شَـرِّ نَفْسِي، وَمِنْ شَـرِّ كُلِّ دَابَّةٍ أَنْـتَ آخِـذٌ
بِنَاصِيَتِهَـا، إِنَّ رَبِّي عَلَـى صِرَاطٍ مُسْتَقِيـمٍ * يَا حَـيُّ يَا قَيُّـومُ، بِرَحْمَتِـكَ
أَسْتَغِيـثُ، وَمِـنْ عَذَابِكَ أَسْتَجِيرُ، أَصْلِـحْ لِي شَـأْنِي كُلَّـهُ، وَلا تَكِلْنِـي إِلى
نَفْسِي ولا إِلَى أَحَـدٍ مِـنْ خَلْقِكَ طَرْفَةَ عَيْنٍ * اللّهُـمَّ إِنِّي أَعُـوذُ بِـكَ
مِـنَ الْهَـمِّ وَالْحَـزَنِ، وَأَعُـوذُ بِـكَ مِـنَ الْعَجْـزِ وَالْكَسَلِ، وَأَعُـوذُ بِـكَ مِـنَ
الْجُـبْنِ وَالْبُخْـلِ، وَأَعُـوذُ بِـكَ مِـنْ غَلَبَـةِ الدَّيْـنِ، وَقَهْرِ الرِّجَالِ * اللّهُـمَّ
إِنِّـي أَسْأَلُـكَ الْعَفْـوَ وَالعافيةَ والـمُعَافَاةَ الدَّائِمَةَ فِي دِينِي وَدُنْيَايَ وَأَهْلِي
وَمَالِـي * اللّهُـمَّ اسْتُرْ عَوْرَاتِي وَآمِنْ رَوْعَاتِي * اللّهُـمَّ احْفَظْنِي مِـنْ بَـيْنِ
يَـدَيَّ وَمِـنْ خَلْفِـي وَعَـنْ يَمِينِـي وَعَـنْ شِمَالِي ، وَمِـنْ فَوْقِـي ، وَأَعُـوذُ
بِعَظَمَتِـكَ أَنْ أُغْتَـالَ مِـنْ تَحْتِـي * اللّهُـمَّ أَنـتَ خَلَقْتَنِـي وَأَنـتَ تَهْدِينِـي
وَأَنـتَ تُطْعِمُنِـي وَأَنـتَ تَسْقِينِـي ، وَأَنـتَ تُمِيتُنِـي وَأَنـتَ تُحْيِينِـي *
أَصْبَحْنَـا عَلَـى فِطْـرَةِ الْإِسْـلامِ، وَعَلَى كَلِمَـةِ الْإِخْـلاصِ، وَعَلَى دِينِ نَبِيِّنَا
مُحَمَّـدٍ، صَلَّى اللهُ عَلَيْـهِ وَآلِـهِ وَسَلَّـمَ، وَعَلَى مِلَّةِ أَبِينَا إِبْرَاهِيمَ، حَنِيفاً
مُسْلِماً، وَمَا كَانَ مِنَ الـمُشْرِكِينَ * اللّهُـمَّ بِكَ أَصْبَحْنَا، وَبِكَ أَمْسَيْنا، وَبِكَ
نَحْيَا وَبِكَ نَمُوتُ، وَإِلَـيْكَ النُّشُورُ * أَصْبَحْنَا وَأَصْبَحَ الـمُلْكُ للهِ، الْحَمْدُ
للهِ رَبِّ الْعَالَمِينَ * اللّهُـمَّ إِنِّي أَسْأَلُكَ خَيـرَ هَـذَا الْيَـوْمِ ، وَنَصْرَهُ ،
وَنُـورَهُ ، وَبَرَكَتَـهُ ، وَهُـدَاهُ * اللّهُـمَّ إِنِّي أَسْأَلُكَ خَيْـرَ هَـذَا الْيَـوْمِ وَخَيْـرَ مَا
فِيـهِ ، وَأَعُـوذُ بِـكَ مِـنْ شَـرِّ هَـذَا الْيَـوْمِ وشَـرِّ مَا فِيهِ * اللّهُـمَّ مَا أَصْبَـحَ
بِي مِـنْ نِعْمَـةٍ أَوْ بِأَحَـدٍ مِـنْ خَلْقِـكَ فَمِنْكَ وَحْـدَكَ لَا شَرِيكَ لَكَ، فَلَكَ

الْحَمْدُ وَلَكَ الشُّكْرُ عَلَى ذلِك * سُبْحَانَ اللَّه وَبِحَمْده (مائة مرّة) * سُبْحَانَ اللّه الْعَظِيم وَبِحَمْده (مائة مرّة) * سُبْحَانَ اللّه، وَالْحَمْدُ للّه، وَلَا إِلَهَ إِلَّا اللَّهُ، وَاللَّهُ أَكْبَرُ (مائة مرة) * وَيَزِيدُ صَبَاحاً : لَا إِلَهَ إِلَّا اللَّهُ وَحْدَهُ لَا شَرِيكَ لَهُ، لَهُ الْمُلْكُ وَلَهُ الْحَمْدُ، وَهُوَ عَلَى كُلِّ شَيْءٍ قَدِيرٌ (مائة مرّة) *

وَيَقُولُ فِي الْمَسَاءِ
بَدَل أَصْبَحْت : أَمْسَيت
وَبَدَل النُّشور : الْمَصير

ARABIC APPANEDIX II:
Al-Ratib al-Shahir

الرَّاتب الشَّهير

بِسْمِ اللَّهِ الرَّحْمَٰنِ الرَّحِيمِ (١)
ٱلْحَمْدُ لِلَّهِ رَبِّ ٱلْعَٰـلَمِينَ (٢) ٱلرَّحْمَٰنِ ٱلرَّحِيمِ (٣) مَٰلِكِ
يَوْمِ ٱلدِّينِ (٤) إِيَّاكَ نَعْبُدُ وَإِيَّاكَ نَسْتَعِينُ (٥) ٱهْدِنَا ٱلصِّرَٰطَ
ٱلْمُسْتَقِيمَ (٦) صِرَٰطَ ٱلَّذِينَ أَنْعَمْتَ عَلَيْهِمْ غَيْرِ ٱلْمَغْضُوبِ عَلَيْهِمْ
وَلَا ٱلضَّآلِّينَ (٧)

ٱللَّهُ لَا إِلَٰهَ إِلَّا هُوَ ٱلْحَيُّ ٱلْقَيُّومُ لَا تَأْخُذُهُ سِنَةٌ وَلَا نَوْمٌ لَّهُ
مَا فِي ٱلسَّمَٰوَٰتِ وَمَا فِي ٱلْأَرْضِ مَن ذَا ٱلَّذِي يَشْفَعُ عِندَهُ إِلَّا بِإِذْنِهِ
يَعْلَمُ مَا بَيْنَ أَيْدِيهِمْ وَمَا خَلْفَهُمْ وَلَا يُحِيطُونَ بِشَيْءٍ مِّنْ عِلْمِهِ
إِلَّا بِمَا شَآءَ وَسِعَ كُرْسِيُّهُ ٱلسَّمَٰوَٰتِ وَٱلْأَرْضَ وَلَا يَئُودُهُ حِفْظُهُمَا
وَهُوَ ٱلْعَلِيُّ ٱلْعَظِيمُ (٢٥٥)

ءَامَنَ ٱلرَّسُولُ بِمَآ أُنزِلَ إِلَيْهِ مِن رَّبِّهِ وَٱلْمُؤْمِنُونَ كُلٌّ ءَامَنَ
بِٱللَّهِ وَمَلَٰٓئِكَتِهِ وَكُتُبِهِ وَرُسُلِهِ لَا نُفَرِّقُ بَيْنَ أَحَدٍ مِّن رُّسُلِهِ وَقَالُوا

سَـمِعْنَا وَأَطَعْنَا غُفْرَانَكَ رَبَّنَا وَإِلَيْكَ ٱلْمَصِيرُ (٢٨٥) لَا يُكَلِّفُ ٱللَّهُ نَفْسًا إِلَّا وُسْعَهَا لَهَا مَا كَسَبَتْ وَعَلَيْهَا مَا ٱكْتَسَبَتْ رَبَّنَا لَا تُؤَاخِذْنَـآ إِن نَّسِينَآ أَوْ أَخْطَأْنَا رَبَّنَا وَلَا تَحْمِلْ عَلَيْنَـآ إِصْرًا كَـمَا حَمَلْتَهُ عَلَى ٱلَّذِينَ مِـن قَبْلِنَا رَبَّنَا وَلَا تُحَمِّلْنَا مَا لَا طَاقَةَ لَنَا بِهِ وَٱعْفُ عَنَّا وَٱغْفِرْ لَنَا وَٱرْحَمْنَـآ أَنتَ مَوْلَـٰنَا فَٱنصُرْنَا عَلَى ٱلْقَوْمِ ٱلْكَـٰفِرِينَ (٢٨٦)

لَا إِلَهَ إِلَّا اللَّهُ وَحْدَهُ لَا شَرِيكَ لَهُ، لَهُ الـمُلْكُ وَلَهُ الحَمْدُ، يُحْيِي وَيُمِيتُ وَهُوَ عَلَى كُلِّ شَيْءٍ قَدِيرٌ (ثلاثاً) * سُبْحَانَ اللهِ، وَالْحَمْدُ لِلَّهِ، وَلَا إِلَهَ إِلَّا اللَّهُ، وَاللَّهُ أَكْبَر (ثلاثاً) * سُبْحَانَ اللَّهِ وَبِحَمْدِهِ، سُـبْحَانَ اللَّهِ الْعَظِيمِ (ثلاثاً) * رَبَّنَا اغْفِرْ لَنَا وَتُبْ عَلَيْنَا،إِنَّكَ أَنْتَ التَّوَّابُ الرَّحِيمُ (ثلاثاً) * اَللَّهُمَّ صَلِّ عَلَى مُحَمَّد، اللَّهُـمَّ صَلِّ عَلَيْهِ وَسَلِّم (ثلاثاً) * أَعوذُ بِكَلِمَاتِ اللَّهِ التَّامَّاتِ مِـن شَرِّ مَا خَلَقَ(ثلاثاً) * بِسم اللَّهِ الَّذِي لَا يَضُرُّ مَعَ اسْمِهِ شَيٌّ فِي الأَرْضِ وَلَا فِي السَّمَاءِ، وَهُـوَ السَّـمِيعُ العَلِيمُ (ثلاثاً) * رَضِينَا بِاللهِ رَبَّـاً وَبِالإِسْلَام دِينا وَبِـمُحَمَّد نَبِيَّا (ثلاثاً) * بِسم اللَّه، وَالْحَمْـدُ لِلَّه، والخَيْرُ والشَّرُّ بِمَشِيئَة اللَّه (ثلاثاً) * آمَنَّا بِاللَّه وَالْيَوْمِ الآخِرْ، تُبْنَا إلى اللَّه بَاطِناً وَظَاهِـرْ (ثلاثاً) * يَا رَبَّنَا وَاعْفُ عَنَّا، وَامْحُ الـَّذِي كَانَ مِنَّا (ثلاثاً) * يَـاذَا الجَـلَالِ وَالإِكْرَامِ، أَمِتْنَـا عَلَى دِينِ الإِسْلام (سبعاً) * يَا قَـوِيُّ يَا مَتِين، اِكْـفِ شَرَّ الظَّالِمِـين (ثلاثاً) * أَصْلَـحْ اَللَّهُ أُمُورَ الْمُسْـلِمِين، صَرَفَ اللَّهُ شَرَّ الـمُؤْذِين (ثلاثاً) * يَا عَلِيُّ يَا كَبِير، يَا عَلِيمُ يَاَ قَدِير، يَا سَمِيعُ يَا بَصِير، يَا لَطِيفُ يَاَ خَبِير

(ثَلاثاً) * يَا فَارِجَ آلهَـمِّ، يَا كَاشِفَ الغَـمِّ، يَا مَـنْ لِعَبْدِهِ يَغْفِرُ
وَيَرْحَـمُ (ثلاثاً) *

أَسْتَغْفِرُ آللهَ رَبَّ البَرَايَا، أَسْتَغْفِرُ آللهَ مِـنَ الخَطَايَا (أربعاً) * لا إلهَ
إلَّا اللهُ (خمسـين مـرّةً وإن بَلَغها إلى ألـف كان حسـناً) * مُحَمَّدٌ
رَسُولُ آللهِ، صَلَّى آللهُ عَلَيهِ وَآلهِ وَسَلَّمَ، وَشَرَّفَ وَكَرَّمَ، وَمَجَّدَ
وَعَظَّمَ، وَرَضِيَ آللهُ عَـنْ أَهْلِ بَيْتِهِ الطَّيِّبِيـنَ الطَّاهِرِينَ، وَأَصْحَابِهِ
الأَخْيَارِ الـمُهْتَدِينَ، والتَّابِعِيـنَ لَهُـمْ بِإِحْسَـانٍ إلي يَـومِ الدِّينِ *

بِسْمِ اللهِ الرَّحْمَنِ الرَّحِيمِ

قُلْ هُوَ آللهُ أَحَدٌ (١) آللهُ الصَّمَدُ (٢) لَمْ يَـلِدْ وَلَمْ يُولَـدْ (٣)
وَلَمْ يَكُـن لَّـهُ كُفُـواً أَحَدٌ (٤) (ثلاثاً)

بِسْمِ اللهِ الرَّحْمَنِ الرَّحِيمِ

قُـلْ أَعُوذُ بِـرَبِّ الفَلَـقِ (١) مِـن شَرِّ مَا خَلَـقَ (٢) وَمِن شَرِّ غَاسِـقٍ إذَا
وَقَـبَ (٣) وَمِـن شَرِّ آلنَّفَّـٰـثَـٰـتِ فِي آلعُقَدِ (٤) وَمِن شَرِّ حَاسِـدٍ
إذَا حَسَدَ (٥)

بِسْمِ اللهِ الرَّحْمَنِ الرَّحِيمِ

قُلْ أَعُوذُ بِـرَبِّ آلنَّـاسِ (١) مَلِكِ آلنَّـاسِ (٢) إلَـٰـهِ آلنَّاسِ (٣) مِـن
شَرِّ آلوَسْـوَاسِ آلخَنَّـاسِ (٤) آلَّـذِي يُوَسْوِسُ فِي صُدُورِ آلنَّاسِ (٥) مِنَ
آلْجِنَّـةِ وَآلنَّاسِ (٦)

الفَاتِحَةُ إلي كَافَّة عِبَـاد اللـه الصَّالحِـين ، وَلِوالِدَينـا ، وَجمَيـع المُؤمِنـينَ وَالمُـؤمِنَات وَالـمُسْلِمينَ وَالـمُسْلِمات، أنَّ اللَّـهَ يَغْفِـرُ لهَـمْ وَيَرحَمُهُـم وَيَنفَعُنـا بِأسْرارِهِـم وَبَرَكاتِهِـم .... وَإلي حَـضْرَة النَّبِـيَّ مُحَمَـدٍ صَـلَّى اللَّـهُ عَلَيـهِ وَسَـلَّم*

اللَّهُمَّ إنَّا نَسْألُك رِضَاكَ وَالجَّنة وَنَعُوذُ بِكَ مِن سَخَطِكَ وَالنار*

QASIDA

Should you not gain your wants, my soul, then be not grieved;
But hasten to that banquet which your Lord's bequeathed.

And when a thing for which you ask is slow to come,
Then know that often through delay are gifts received.

Find solace in privation and respect its due,
For only by contentment is the heart relieved.

And know that when the trials of life have rendered you
Despairing of all hope, and of all joy bereaved,

Then shake yourself and rouse yourself from heedlessness,
And make pure hope a meadow that you never leave.

Your Maker's gifts take subtle and uncounted forms.

How fine the fabric of the world His hands have weaved.

The journey done, they came to the water of life,
And all the caravan drank deep, their thirst allieved.

Far be it from the host to leave them thirsty there,
His spring pours forth all generosity received.

My Lord, my trust in all Your purposes is strong,
That trust is now my shield; I'm safe, and undeceived.

All those who hope for grace from You will feel Your rain;
Too generous are You to leave my branch unleaved.

May blessings rest upon the loved one, Muhammad,
Who's been my means to high degrees since I believed.

He is my fortress and my handhold, so my soul,
Hold fast, and travel to a joy still unconceived.

—Imam Ali bin Husayn al-Habshi (translated by Abdal Hakim Murad)